Real-Life Problem Solving

A Collaborative Approach to Interdisciplinary Learning

Series Titles

Real-Life Problem Solving

A Collaborative Approach to Interdisciplinary Learning

Beau Fly Jones, Claudette M. Rasmussen, and Mary C. Moffitt

with contributions by
Kim Alamar, Mary Brady, Andree Duggan, Will Duggan, Sheila Epstein,
Sheryl L. Finkle, Paul Gilvary, Ted Injasulian, Susan Kolian, William
Munroe, Sheila Schlaggar, Gail Sims Smith, Linda T. Torp, Delamie
Thompson

AMERICAN PSYCHOLOGICAL ASSOCIATION | WASHINGTON, DC

Published by
American Psychological Association
750 First Street, NE
Washington, DC 20002

Copies may be ordered from
APA Order Department
P.O. Box 92984
Washington, DC 20090-2984

In the UK and Europe, copies may be ordered from
American Psychological Association
3 Henrietta Street
Covent Garden, London
WC2E 8LU England

Typeset in Berkeley and Bell Gothic by University Graphics, Inc., York, PA
Printer: Data Reproductions Corporation, Rochester Hills, MI
Cover Designer: Minker Design, Bethesda, MD
Technical/Production Editor: Edward B. Meidenbauer

Library of Congress Cataloging-in-Publication Data
Jones, Beau Fly.
    Real-life problem solving : a collaborative approach to interdisciplinary
    learning / Beau Fly Jones, Claudette M. Rasmussen, and Mary C. Moffitt.
       p.   cm. — (Psychology in the classroom)
    Includes bibliographical references (p.   ).
    ISBN 1-55798-294-5 (pbk.)
    1.   Interdisciplinary approach in education—United States.   2. Group
work in education—United States.   3. Problem-based learning—United
States.   4. Educational change—United States.   I. Rasmussen, Claudette M.
II. Moffitt, Mary C.   III. Title.   IV. Series.
LB1570.J626   1997
371. 39′5—dc21   96-39391
                                                                CIP

British Library Cataloguing-in-Publication Data
A CIP record is available from the British Library.

Printed in the United States of America
First Edition

We dedicate this book to some of our most important codevelopers.
Jim Davis, Lavern Rasmussen, Russ and Kelsey Katahira, and Jane Friesema
have shared and shaped our lives in so many meaningful ways.

TABLE OF CONTENTS

PREFACE

This book is very special to us. It represents new direction and continued growth not only in our careers as educators, but in those of the teachers, principals, and facilitators who developed this book with us. We believe the knowledge we have gained about interdisciplinary, problem-based learning will be helpful to you, your colleagues, and your students.

We chose the practitioners who wrote the book's problem-based instructional profiles from very different learning contexts: some urban, some suburban; some focused on learning for gifted students, others on learning for students at risk; some projects within one school, some involving multiple schools; some projects with technology, others without. These practitioners also represent very different stages of development. Some had little prior involvement with problem-based learning but were looking for new interdisciplinary approaches; some were very experienced in problem-based learning and were seeking to improve their practice; and still others wished to share their experiences and work with others to apply them in new settings.

This book tells their stories of innovation, of changes in roles and relationships, and of the struggles and triumphs experienced along the way. In many ways, this book reflects the changes in our roles and relationships as we work with interdisciplinary, problem-based innovations.

Although it was never our intent, in the past we often did things somewhat in isolation. Beau Jones, the cognitive researcher on this team, often created books and materials working as a member of a small group that had information and resources to pass along to others. Typically, the authors were all researchers who tried to consider the strengths and perspectives of teachers. Unfortunately, it was becoming clear that the authors were the primary beneficiaries of the process, not the teachers in the field. Teacher-leaders Claudette Rasmussen and Mary Moffitt often created materials out of sheer necessity. They found themselves responding to the immediate needs of the classroom or workshop, trying to provide "just enough, just in time." Whenever possible, they sought out like-minded people as collaborators.

With this book, we combine knowledge and experience from research and practice. We write about sound interdisciplinary practices that support engaged learning. We also saw this as an opportunity to try a new approach to curriculum development and professional development—one that would truly "walk the talk" and model with teachers what we espoused for students. We found that everyone benefits more when the work is codeveloped with the people using it in schools. First, the work is necessarily grounded in the needs and goals of all the participants. Second, various groups and teams can share in solving problems, asking questions, and building knowledge, and each can contribute its unique perspective and resources.

The result of our discovery is that each of the tools in this book was created in response to the needs and ideas of diverse practitioners and their students. The author teams used these tools either to reflect on and evaluate an interdisciplinary unit taught in the past or to design a new problem-based unit of study.

As we prepared to write this book, we reflected on what we thought about teaching and learning. We gradually realized that we were moving from a primary focus on interdisciplinary teaching to a more fundamental focus on interdisciplinary learning in which teachers codevelop units with students. Ultimately, we chose problem-based learning for our focus because we believe it is the most powerful approach for interdisciplinary units. We called our model Problem-Based Learning as Codevelopment (PBL-CD) because of the richness of the experience of working with teachers and others as colearners.

This shift had profound implications for us as researchers, curriculum developers, and facilitators who provide opportunities for professional development. Broadly speaking, it meant that we would shift from learning among ourselves to learning with others, from constructing knowledge to coconstructing it, from making decisions among ourselves to negotiating them with others. We went from supporting teachers as individuals and teams to building communities of practice that would include not only teachers, but also library media specialists, technology coordinators, administrators, practitioners in the field, and community members. Finally, we sought to incorporate meaningful roles into this work for the people most affected by learning and teaching—students.

We hope this book encourages teachers to reflect on their own practice and to codevelop interdisciplinary, problem-based curriculum units with their students and other teachers. We are not asking you to abandon approaches you have developed in the past. Rather, we invite you to build on your strengths by integrating new practices into your approaches and strategies, reflecting on what works and what does not work for you. For some teachers, this may mean choosing to make a bold shift from a more traditional, discipline-based instructional approach to an interdisciplinary, problem-based unit that is codeveloped with other teachers and with students, embedding the best knowledge and skills from previous practice. For others, it may mean identifying one or two elements or activities that fit your style and your students' needs, and exploring how best to incorporate them into your current methods. In both instances, we encourage you to share and reflect on your ideas with others when planning for a curriculum unit, during the actual implementation, and after teaching the unit. This constant refurbishing of your understanding with ideas from multiple perspectives is a give-and-take process that empowers teachers to look to colleagues to help solve problems, share the responsibility for learning, and build community.

Developing this book with others has been among the most liberating and rewarding experiences of our professional lives, and it has deepened our commitment to sharing and negotiating ideas. We are excited about the work and growth we shared together and its impact on students and teachers. This book celebrates the work of these teams.

We invite you to join us in an ever-expanding community of practice around interdisciplinary, problem-based learning.

Beau Fly Jones
Claudette M. Rasmussen
Mary C. Moffitt

ACKNOWLEDGMENTS

This book was produced working with a variety of author teams, most of them in Chicago and nearby cities or suburbs. The teams represent diverse learning contexts and subject area interests. We would like to express here our deepest gratitude to these authors for the opportunity to share in the excitement and risks of moving along new paths, building new visions of learning from shared experiences, and codeveloping tools that are situated in real learning contexts.

We thank these individuals and schools for making the commitment to try a new way and for believing in the work together: (a) Irene DaMota, principal, and Susan Kolian, Kim Alamar, and Sheila Epstein, the fifth grade teacher team at Whittier Elementary School, Chicago; (b) Sheila Schlagger, principal, Gail Smith, library media specialist, and Jack Matsumoto, lead teacher for the multi-grade elementary unit on parallel evolution at Edison Regional Gifted Center, Chicago; (c) principal Gary Moriello, Delamie Thompson, nurse at the Gladstone School and Family Nursing Center, and Paul Gilvary, sixth grade teacher, at Gladstone Elementary in Chicago; (d) Mary Brady and William Munroe, former teachers at Avoca Elementary School District, Wilmette, Illinois; (e) Sheryl Finkle and Linda Torp at the Illinois Mathematics and Science Academy in Aurora, Illinois; and finally, (f) Will Duggan and Andree Duggan, Interactive FrameWorks, Inc., a consulting group near Baltimore, Maryland.

We must also thank Alan Brown, Superintendent, and Elaine Armani, Associate Superintendent for Curriculum and Instruction, Waukegan School District in Illinois for a parallel project to codevelop problem-based learning units in two Waukegan initiatives. The first, Goals 2000, was a statewide effort initiated by the Superintendent to apply concepts of middle school and interdisciplinary, problem-based learning first to six high schools in Illinois who would then mentor up to 30 high schools. The second was a citywide project involving 11 teacher teams (K-12) and three district technology coordinators to develop problem-based learning units that would integrate two or more subjects plus technology. We are indebted to these projects for the opportunity to build communities of practice and codevelop tools related to problem-based learning. We also thank Rita Melius, Abbott Middle School principal; Ted Injasulian, Abbott art teacher; and Jo Williamson, Waukegan middle school technology coordinator, for the codevelopment of an eighth grade sculpture unit for this book.

Additionally, we must thank various reviewers. We are particularly indebted to Carole Fine, at the North Central Regional Educational Laboratory (NCREL), Mary Lamon, Professional Development Researcher, and Todd Fennimore, Ohio Supercomputing Center, for their very valuable comments on parts of this book. We must also thank Tatia Beckwith and Mary Costello, both in the Department of Curriculum and Instruction, Northern Illinois University; and Tom Stefonek, Division for Learning Support, Instructional Services, Wisconsin Department of Public Instruction, for their reviews of earlier drafts.

We are indebted to Angie Liberty, NCREL, for the work she did in the early development of our pictorial scenario and to Terri Williams and Kim Martin of Katapa Art & Design. Final thanks are to Lenaya Raack and Mary Ann Larson, NCREL, for their skill and perseverance in helping us put this book together.

introduction

In Search of More Meaningful Learning and Teaching

"Earlier I used to think about teachable moments. Now I am more often thinking about learnable moments   when we take notice, when we take issue, when we decide, when we coconstruct."

Irene DaMota, Principal, Whittier Elementary School

At last, another hectic school year is drawing to a close. Bill Mundy always forgets just how much material there is to organize and put away.

He thumbs through one of his seventh-grade textbooks before putting it into a cabinet. Bill is pleased that some of the more engaging topics in math, such as probability and geometry, have made their way toward the front of the text. He is also gratified by the increased emphasis on reasoning and problem-solving standards. Still, he muses, few of the text's activities and problems had seemed especially meaningful to his students. But at least some of the end-of-the-unit projects he had designed had captured the students' interest.

Bill notices a crumpled paper sticking out of one of the textbooks: It's Hector's semester score report. Hector was one of those kids who did poorly on tests and showed little motivation for most math activities, even the projects. In fact, he often questioned the relevance of math to his life.

Bill is bothered that the majority of Hector's grade was based on his chapter test performance. He doesn't feel that the grade is a true representation of Hector's abilities. Although Bill had used some performance-based assessments for project work this year, he hadn't given them much weight in his overall grading. He still isn't sure how to justify the value of such nontraditional measures to administrators and parents.

It really troubles Bill that he had not been able to "hook" Hector on the importance of math. He can't help but question: Is he really focusing on the skills most needed by his students? Is he actually preparing them for "real life"?

Bill's colleague, Carmen Delgado, enters his classroom, providing him with a welcome diversion. Knowing that Carmen regularly used hands-on activities with her sixth-grade math students, Bill tells how his students Mercedes and Talia had invented a game, demonstrating a genuine understanding of odds. Their enthusiasm had spread throughout the class. Recalling this, Bill states that he is more certain than ever that student-created projects and original experiments need to be an integral part of his curriculum.

Carmen agrees and notes that her students had transferred the problem-solving approach they used in student-designed measurement experiments to the scientific thinking they used in the Invention Convention. Bill is curious about her success in integrating language arts activities into the science unit. Carmen says that it was very helpful to have the speech and writing research units coincide with the Invention Convention. The students felt a genuine need to write in-depth reports and refine their speeches because they actually used them in their presentations to judges.

Bill is excited to think that he will be receiving students next year who have experienced interdisciplinary work and have transferred their thinking across subject areas. When Carmen hurries off, Bill begins considering the possibilities: What will he have to do to build on such connections? How can he be more student-centered rather than test and text driven? What kinds of interdisciplinary things can he and his colleagues do? How can they be sure that the required curriculum standards are met?

Bill comes across an article on "real-life" problem solving in the middle school math journal. Skimming it, he sees that other teachers have similar questions related to making learning more relevant for students. It also seems as if studying problems based on questions generated with students is a more powerful teaching and learning approach. Although Bill feels good about his focus on projects involving problem solving, this article makes him realize that there is a distinct difference in using thought-provoking word problems and hands-on projects versus having students work to solve authentic problems.

Bill thinks back to Mercedes and Talia. Inventing a game was more than a hands-on activity for them, it was an authentic task! He remembered how clearly and confidently the two girls had explained the logic of the game to their peers.

Maybe more authentic problem solving would have finally gotten Hector invested in his own learning. It might even have stopped his "What's this got to do with real life?" question!

Bill suddenly realizes that it is *that very question* that could guide his own learning and teaching. Office cleaning forgotten, he excitedly writes down some of the questions, ideas, and insights that have been on his mind today.

Feeling a certain sense of accomplishment, Bill chooses some resources from his piles and shoves the remaining items into a nearby cabinet. These will just have to wait until August. Bill closes his classroom door and walks down the now empty hall. He smiles. After all, it is the beginning of the long-awaited summer. And although Bill has more questions now, they are ones that excite rather than perplex him.

LOOKING FORWARD: PROBLEM-BASED LEARNING AS CODEVELOPMENT

Although the scenario above is fiction, it echoes the experiences of teachers everywhere. It is often not until the school year's end that teachers have sufficient time to look back on what worked and what did not work, as well as to consider ways to make learning and teaching more meaningful. Many reflective practitioners see limitations to instruction founded largely on textbooks. They have been searching for and experimenting with instructional strategies and approaches that are interdisciplinary and collaborative, involve student-generated problems and solutions, focus on authentic tasks and interactive projects, use performance-based assessments, and link to broader standards.

Of the many promising choices and directions for teachers like Bill and Carmen, we believe that interdisciplinary, problem-based learning is one of the most powerful approaches. It offers teachers the means both to address their questions and to make learning and teaching more meaningful for them and their students.

In problem-based learning (PBL), teachers and students integrate concepts and skills from one or more disciplines while investigating a problem. PBL often engages students in the development of a relatively long-term project.

As it is defined in the research literature and in its best practice, PBL goes beyond the typical interdisciplinary hands-on projects taught in many schools. Typically, such projects focus on general themes such as "Minnesota," "Exploration," or "Primates," and involve students in research on various topics or categories of information such as "characteristics of primates." The themes and subtopics are usually identified by the teacher. We refer to such thematic projects as *project-based teaching* (Jones, Rasmussen, & Moffitt, 1996). In contrast, projects such as "What kind of pollution is killing some lakes in Minnesota?" or "What capacity do primates have for language?" are focused on problems. These projects have two essential features, as defined by Blumenfeld, Soloway, Marx, Krajik, Guzdial, and Palincsar (1991): (a) questions or problems organize and drive activities in the classroom, and (b) these activities lead to various artifacts or products that culminate in a final product that addresses the driving questions. We consider project-based learning that results from projects focused on problems to be synonymous with *problem-based learning.*

Our model, Problem-Based Learning as Codevelopment (PBL-CD), supports such problem-based learning in very specific ways as described in chapters 2 and 3. Further, we emphasize that PBL involves codeveloping ideas and materials both for teachers and students. The PBL-CD model itself was developed in collaboration with teachers, library media specialists, and technology specialists from several elementary and high schools. We believe its major strengths lie in this codevelopment and in the fact that it is a synthesis of concepts and processes from research and best practice on learning.

It will be helpful to illustrate our model by continuing our scenario, approximately 18 months later, to show what might occur as Bill and Carmen integrate elements of PBL-CD into their classrooms and as their school moves forward with interdisciplinary, problem-based learning and teaching.

> During the past school year, Carmen and her colleague Eric Shaw, a language arts teacher, had actively sought out information about interdisciplinary, problem-based learning. They had even visited other schools where students were investigating real-life problems. Bill, meanwhile, had made it his professional goal to learn everything he could about authentic problem-solving experiences. These three, along with Coretta Wills, a social studies teacher, had been among the pioneers in their school to write problem-based learn-

ing units during the recent summer while working with curriculum consultants. Now, there are a number of teams throughout the school exploring interdisciplinary problem-based learning. This work is part of a year-long commitment all teams have made to codevelop curricula with each other and with the consultants.

As the principal, Beverly, makes her rounds of the classrooms, she sees a rich array of activities that demonstrate progress toward implementing problem-based learning. With interest, she observes Bill and Carmen as they team-teach a unit on local conservation issues. They move about the class sometimes listening to, sometimes talking with student work groups that are planning guidelines for collaborative work. Beverly smiles as she watches Carmen work with a group of students to generate criteria for self-assessment. She and her students have discovered the power of codeveloping assessment criteria from the very beginning of a unit. And Bill seems energized now that he can give students more opportunities to pursue problems of importance to them. As he monitors the small groups' work, he occasionally poses a guiding question to prompt student planning.

When the activity has finished, the team makes an appointment with Beverly to review further their plans for this problem-based learning unit. Beverly feels good that she and the teachers found a way to change the schedule to allow for common planning time dedicated to developing these units for the teachers, even though it meant her taking lunchroom supervision each week. She has promised to meet with each interdisciplinary teacher team so that she can help align curricular outcomes and assessments and lend support in any other way she can.

Beverly's next stop is Coretta and Eric's classroom. Their students are in the middle of a debriefing. As Beverly watches, the class generates a concept map representing what they have learned about bridging cultural differences within their community. She recalls last week's student presentations, part of the multicultural exhibit at the local library. The students had made their presentations first to other students in the class and the school, then to library staff, parents, and community members. It was clear that both the presentations and this debriefing resulted in new insights for the students.

At one time, Beverly had thought that a final presentation and its assessment was the demonstration of learning. Listening to these children, she now realizes that valuable knowledge building results from summarizing collectively what has been learned, even after assessment of small group presentations. Students seem to consolidate learning as they reflect upon and refine their earlier hypotheses and consider the implications of their findings.

Following class, Beverly shares this insight with Coretta and Eric. They, in turn, share the development of the debriefing process with her. They explain that they had, in fact, given their unit plans to Bill and Carmen for a critical review. This "critical friend" team had helped to refine their debriefing process with the students. Beverly recalls how energized all the teacher teams were when reviewing and collaborating on each other's plans. She had worried that some teams would not set aside

time to continue this codevelopment
process once the school year was underway, but so far they had. We have all come
a long way, Beverly mused. . . .

Bill has indeed come a long way since he was prompted
by Hector's crumpled report to question how his teaching
might support more meaningful learning. His colleagues
and their principal, Beverly, have also come a long way in
their understanding of the power of authentic problem
solving to engage students and enhance their learning.
Their commitment to codeveloping PBL curricula has involved them in new roles that mirror those of their students. The students' new roles were as coevaluators (they
developed and used assessment criteria), and coplanners
and coproducers (they designed and developed their own
presentations). Following in their students' footsteps, the
educators became colearners, coproducers, and coevaluators as they designed, implemented, and continually refined their curricula.

These experiences, as described in our scenarios, represent a composite of the rich, field-based experiences we
have had during the evolution of this book and a parallel
book we codeveloped with high school teachers (Jones, Rasmussen, & Moffitt, 1996). Throughout our process of examining the research on learning, of negotiating and codeveloping the PBL-CD model with practitioners in schools, and
of observing the impact of authentic problem solving on
teachers and students, we, too, have come a long way.

Our PBL-CD model and its approach to curriculum development, professional development, and the ways in
which engaged learning takes place in the classroom reflect
a fundamental shift—from a focus on teaching to a focus
on learning and codeveloping. Our model is grounded in
a solid understanding of the research on learning and the
ways in which teaching can support more meaningful
learning. It is also grounded in best practice—the experi-
ence-based wisdom of educators in schools that recognizes,
among other things, the significance of the "learnable moments" and the power of coconstructing.

ORGANIZATION OF THIS BOOK

We wrote this book for practitioners who, as part of their own professional growth, are interested in examining learning environments and codeveloping curricula that are both interdisciplinary *and* problem based. We have organized the material in a manner that is supportive of such self-study and independent codevelopment. Readers will want to pay special attention to the guided self-study questions at the end of each section. These questions can be used to make the important link between research and practice. The self-study activities are intended to engage readers in a progressive problem-solving process that encourages them to think about the material by planning an application, acting on their plan, sharing their results, reflecting on their work, and rethinking and refining the work. In these activities we ask that you share your work with one or more critical friends. The role of critical friends is to provide helpful feedback and to stimulate further reflection and refinement of work. Critical friends can become significant codevelopers.

We use stories about practice to ground our research and to bring the struggles and triumphs of teachers and students to life. Some of the stories are fiction, such as the representative scenarios you have read in this chapter; others are real-life examples of PBL described by us in Goal 1 and by practitioners in upcoming Goals 4–7.

We have also included a number of items that support interdisciplinary, problem-based learning and codevelopment in the appendices: indicators of engaged learning, a template for aligning curricular outcomes with assessments within a PBL unit, and a detailed illustration of the teaching and learning process as it might play out in a classroom over the course of a PBL-CD unit.

This book, like others in the series, is organized in terms of goals rather than chapters. In Goal 1, we present various strands of research as well as different models of PBL that address why interdisciplinary, problem-based learning approaches are important. In Goal 2, we look at what our model is by examining the features of PBL-CD. Goal 3 describes our model in more depth, focusing on the codevelopment process—how teacher teams codevelop PBL curricula and how teachers and students engage in codevelopment throughout a problem-based unit.

Goals 4 to 7 contain Profiles developed by author teams working on specific problem-based learning units. The author teams represent diverse learning contexts: some urban, some suburban; some focused on learning for gifted students, others on learning for students at risk; some projects within one school, some involving multiple schools; some projects with technology, others without.

These instructional Profiles reflect where teachers were pedagogically when they worked on these units. In some cases, the unit had already been taught and the Profile is a reflective look back at how it could be enhanced using our model of problem-based learning as codevelopment. In other cases, the model was used to design units to be taught. In still other cases, the unit was designed, developed, and taught over the course of the project. Some units are very polished, having been taught more than once. A few of our Profiles are more like pilot studies more exploratory, with clear goals not fully defined.

Problem-based learning, as we have defined it, is an iterative process aimed at continual refinement. We feel that it is important to provide case studies that were in beginning stages as well as those more refined through reflection and practice. Further, we believe these Profiles represent the range of readiness for PBL CD of our readers and that both novices and experts can benefit from this book.

In the course of developing these Profiles, many of the author teams engaged in informal action research. They asked research-based questions of interest to them, designed activities to address the questions, and made observations that informed their theories of learning and their practice. Two Profiles apply some ideas from the multiple intelligences concept; two examine aspects of multicultural research; two incorporate elements of community service or service learning research; one discusses project-enhanced science learning; and two provide additional research on problem-based learning. We believe that all of these Profiles represent an innovative genre in the areas of curriculum and professional development. They have some of the messiness and struggles of a case study, but the applied research adds a discipline and perspective to the thinking and writing that are often absent from case studies. These Profiles speak from the heart and the mind as well as from best practice and research. We believe that there is enough substance in each Profile for readers to be able to apply the ideas to their own learning contexts.

GOALS FOR THE READERS OF THIS BOOK

This is truly a book written *for* practitioners in codevelopment *with* practitioners. We hope that you will find both meaning and community in reading this book. As you interact with this material, we hope that you and your colleagues will work together to accomplish your personal goals as well as the goals we have outlined below:

1. To understand the features of Problem-Based Learning as Codevelopment. This also means understanding how principles of learning guide the teaching-learning process in the schools and the curriculum development process.

2. To recognize the importance and nature of progressive problem solving as it applies to learning and to professional development.

3. To understand the codevelopment process as it occurs between teachers and students in schools, within practitioner teams, and among practitioner teams, professional developers, and the broader research and development community.

4. To understand the power of communities of practice that provide diverse relationships, multiple perspectives, and shared goals and resources for teaching and learning.

5. To appreciate a range of applications of interdisciplinary, problem-based learning.

6. To reflect on your own practice and engage in planning for problem-based teaching and learning.

1 **Understanding and Planning**: In the opening scenario to this chapter, Bill's reflections upon past practice helped him to clarify ways to make learning and teaching more meaningful in his classroom. We invite you to identify further instructional needs by looking back on your own practice. Use the following set of questions to build upon your understanding of your students and their needs and interests.

Consider your classroom. What students and experiences are memorable—both the successful and not-so-successful?

What insights, concerns, and questions did they raise?

How did you respond?

Recognizing that change is a personal and ongoing process, which of your practices are you truly ready to change?

---

2 **Acting and Sharing**: Think about how to make your practices more interdisciplinary and problem-based. Describe your ideas below. Also think about the nature of these changes and how you might cope with them. Share your ideas and feelings with a critical friend, much as Bill and Carmen and Coretta and Eric did in their roles as critical friend teams for one another.

3 **Reflecting**: Reflect upon the ideas and feelings shared with and by your critical friends. List or in some way represent them (metaphor, graphic organizer, icon).

4 **Rethinking and Refining**: What are the implications for you and your colleagues? How do you intend to be more responsive to student needs? In what ways will changes to your practice reflect more interdisciplinary, problem-based practices?

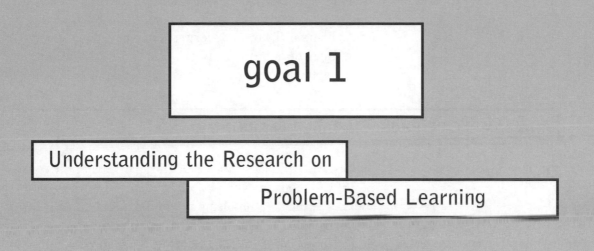

goal 1

Understanding the Research on
Problem-Based Learning

Bill and Carmen, the reflective practitioners in the Introduction, illustrated a need for interdisciplinary, problem-based learning (PBL). We used Bill, Carmen, and their colleagues to represent some ways in which Problem-Based Learning as Codevelopment (PBL-CD) makes learning and teaching more meaningful. In this chapter, we use a real-life example of PBL and the social processes that move investigations forward.

We begin with an overview of Berenfeld's (1993) study of Pease Middle School in San Antonio, Texas. We elaborate on that example as we discuss specific aspects of the research and make the case for PBL. Following that, we explore different approaches to PBL. Finally, we show how PBL-CD represents research and relates to other approaches.

AN EXAMPLE OF PROBLEM-BASED LEARNING

At Pease Middle School, students participated in the Global Lab program, which allows students to work as scientists, sharing their problems and findings with other students around the country as well as with experts in the field. Global Lab is one of the many problem-based curricular programs focusing on the study of the environment and conservation developed by TERC, a Boston research-based group that develops scientific technologies for use in schools. As part of this project, students used an inexpensive air pump designed by TERC to investigate the question, "How safe is the air we breathe?" Because school policy prohibited Pease students from going into the outside environment to collect a variety of air samples, they measured the air inside their classroom and school, found too much CO_2, and concluded that the school had a pollution problem. The school called the local Environmental Protection Agency and officials came out to measure the quality of the air. Using their own expensive equipment, EPA officials confirmed the students' measurements. Students at Pease communicated both sets of findings using the Internet and the Global Lab database to students in other parts of the United States and the world.

Students from a school in South Carolina reviewed the data from the Pease students and designed a study to test the hypothesis that excessive CO_2 was a pollution problem. They compared air samples in regular and mobile classrooms, expecting the latter to be worse because the mobile units were smaller than most classrooms and needed a separate generator for climate control. Instead, they found the opposite. The levels of CO_2 were lower in the mobile units. The students wondered why and posed this problem to other students and scientists on the Global Lab Network.

As part of the conversations among the participating schools and practicing scientists, the students from South Carolina and from Texas came to understand that the excessive CO_2 was a ventilation problem, not a pollution problem. Apparently opening the doors brought fresh air into mobile unit classrooms, lowering the level of CO_2.

Their conversations with local officials and with scientists also gave them new roles and ways of thinking about themselves as learners, researchers, and experts on a local environmental problem. And although their investigation was science-based, it incorporated many cross-curricular thinking and communication skills.

This example illustrates the importance of meaningful conversation about the conceptual content under investigation and of knowledge building in which the data and perspectives each individual or group contributes enrich the whole community of learners (Scardamalia & Bereiter, 1992). Of course, such knowledge building can occur with little or no technology. In fact, the students at Pease Middle School had only one computer in the classroom.

THE CASE FOR PROBLEM-BASED LEARNING

Bridges and Hallinger (1992) identify three grounds for using problem-based learning: cognitive, motivational, and functional. In the sections below, we examine these broad premises generally and in relation to the example above.

Cognitive

We will review briefly some of the strands of research on cognitive development and the ways in which they support engaged learning. The research on comprehension and learning within the cognitive sciences reveals that rote learning may be effective in the short run for many routine tasks and tests, but it is not effective for deep understanding and retention of complex information or problem solving. Thus, students may have knowledge that they cannot access, a widespread phenomenon called inert knowledge (e.g., The Cognition and Technology Group at Vanderbilt, 1992). Most cognitive scientists believe that learners must interact with the ideas in context to make sense of the problem or task. Learners must work actively to construct meaning through internal dialogue and thinking processes or through interaction with others to achieve deep comprehension for text-based activities and problem solving. Unfortunately, the kinds of instructional activities used in many schools today do not meet the conditions for learning that engage students' minds. In contrast, in PBL approaches, because the context of learning is similar to the context of actual use, both retention and functional use improve. In a word, students are much more likely to achieve deep understanding of what they learn in PBL approaches. This is one reason why PBL students perform well on both standardized and alternative assessments, even when there has been no instructional focus on the isolated facts and skills on the tests. These findings are typical of problem-based learning with computer-supported technology and without it. (See citations throughout this chapter. See also Jones, Valdez, Nowakowski, & Rasmussen, 1995, for a synthesis of research on engaged learning and technology, which includes most features of problem-based learning.)

Brooks and Brooks (1993) have synthesized the cognitive research in their principles of constructivist classrooms. According to these authors, constructivism values (a) a curriculum focus moving from whole to part with an emphasis on big concepts, and curricular activities using primary source data and manipulative materials; (b) the role of the student as thinker with emerging theories of the world working in collaboration with others; (c) teacher roles that mediate the learning environment and value student questions and points of view; and (d) assessment that is ongoing and integrated with student learning with a focus on teacher observations, student exhibitions, and portfolios. Many, if not most, problem-based approaches have been derived largely from this broader constructivist philosophy.

In the Pease Middle School example, much of the instruction and activity was focused on the problem of air quality in a given environment and how it can be improved. Clearly the students' questions were valued. Teachers mediated the learning environment by helping students set up experiments that would test their emerging theories and by guiding them to a new understanding through meaningful dialogue. Students and teachers made ongoing assessments from the first set of air quality measurements through the EPA verification of those original measurements and the use of those findings for subsequent experimentation.

Another strand of research—the theory of multiple intelligences developed by Gardner in *Frames of Mind* (1993) and other works—suggests that the traditional methods of formal instruction are not consistent with what we know about the nature and development of intelligence. This theory proposes that the intelligences that are primarily developed in schools—verbal-linguistic and mathematical-deductive reasoning—are not necessarily what it takes to succeed in life. According to Gardner, there are at least five other intelligences that are valued by society: kinesthetic, spatial, musical, interpersonal, and intrapersonal. Learners can be very bright, yet lack the interpersonal and intrapersonal skills to be successful and productive.

Problem-based learning develops social and intrapersonal skills in several ways. Students typically work in groups that, over time, may be very self-organizing and directed. Their frequent interactions with peers, various teachers, community members, and experts develop additional communication and problem-solving skills. Intrapersonal skills are developed through various opportunities to reflect on the work through journals, decisions about self-assessments, selections for portfolios, periodic debriefing, and challenging ideas from others. Because problem-based learning students are typically engaged in hands-on activities and graphic or pictorial representations of their understanding, kinesthetic and spacial learning is reinforced.

Most of these elements were present in the Pease Middle School example. Also, the museum project Profile in Goal 5 involves defining problem-based activities for multiple intelligences.

There is much in brain-based research that supports using problem-based learning in the classroom. Caine and Caine (1994), for example, discuss the concept of downshifting: the notion that when an individual perceives a situation as threatening, he or she essentially regresses to earlier, more primitive habits of mind. The focus in American schools on round-robin reading, especially for older students, and high-stakes, norm-referenced testing used in placement decisions and often published in district and state reports is very threatening. Further, the search for meaning occurs through seeking and finding patterns. Thus, students may have a high "time on task," but if the task is busywork or drill and practice, they are not likely to be learning because the work is not challenging, is done outside of meaningful contexts, or involves information isolated from principles of deeper understanding.

Additionally, Sylwester (1995) argues that the new theories of the electrical basis of the brain suggest that classrooms that promote learning would (a) focus more on drawing out existing skills and knowledge rather than on precisely measuring success with imposed skills; (b) encourage personal (student-generated) construction of categories rather than imposing existing categorical systems; and (c) emphasize narrative information over expository text.

In problem-based learning, the work is typically very exciting and minimally threatening because the students help each other, the teacher acts as facilitator and colearner, and assessments are more meaningful and used primarily to monitor progress. Moreover, PBL is consistent with brain-based learning because there is so much emphasis on student-generated construction of categories, problem formulation, hypotheses, and solutions. These conditions were present in the Pease Middle School example.

We think that PBL is more closely aligned with the new thinking in science, articulated so eloquently by Wheatley (1992). She studied the dramatic new ideas that are emerging from quantum physics, recent research on cellular biology and the brain, and other new science approaches. In the past, scientific views of causation were simplistic: A causes B, or A and other factors interact to cause B. Now we understand that causation is often unpredictable and nonlinear with the same factor being both cause and effect.

In the Pease Middle School example, students were constantly engaged in conversations that challenged their thinking and provided multiple perspectives related to their hypotheses and procedures. Teachers and scientists were there to guide their thinking. In most classrooms, the investigation might have ended once the students determined that there was too much CO_2 in the air. Instead, students at Pease learned to think more deeply about causation and problem formulation. Also in the Pease example, the context for learning was rich with graphic representations generated by students (e.g., charts showing the air samples from various locations), with challenging analysis and guidance from diverse social interactions, and with new roles for students and teachers (colearners and coinvestigators). It is not surprising that students' learning is better retained and concepts more deeply understood using problem-based learning, compared with traditional textbook approaches or less powerful hands-on experiences.

In many ways student learning at Pease Middle School reflects the increasing consensus about what defines highly engaged and meaningful learning. There have been numerous efforts to capture the common elements of engaged learning in research syntheses and principles of learning that cut across strands of cognitive research: for example, the learner-centered principles developed by the American Psychological Association Presidential Task Force on Psychology and Education (1993); the principles for constructivist learning developed by Brooks and Brooks (1993); and the indicators of reform instruction articulated by Means and her colleagues (1993).

We have built upon these and the key variables of learning and instruction described by Jones (1992) to create the Indicators of Engaged Learning included in Appendix A. These 26 Indicators further define 8 broad variables of learning: vision of learning, tasks, assessment, instructional model, learning context, grouping, teacher roles, and student roles (Jones, Valdez, Nowakowski, & Rasmussen, 1995). These Indicators of Engaged Learning have been a helpful guide to many practitioners when analyzing current instruction and planning for future teaching and learning. In fact, several of the authors of the Profiles in Goals 4 to 7 incorporated the Indicators in their planning and self-assessment. PBL, in general, and PBL-CD, in particular, exemplify engaged learning according to these Indicators.

Motivational

PBL is highly motivating both for students and teachers (see also Blumenfeld et al., 1991). Because student work focuses on problems, issues, and questions they create, students have more choices, more ownership. Because they play such a role in designing the research, resources, and assessments, the work is engaging, often exciting, and it develops talents. Also, working with experts, policymakers, and community members as mentors, role models, and colearners demonstrates to students that their work and education are valued by significant people and that it is well-aligned to real world needs. Assessments are often as interesting and fun as other activities. Moreover, because the criteria and the format of the demonstrations are well-known in advance, there is less cause for test anxiety. Teacher roles are more supportive and nurturing, compared with traditional instruction. Finally, working with the networked technologies associated with many PBL approaches is a powerful incentive to many students, enabling them to collaborate with others, locally and globally, to solve real-life problems of common interest.

In the Pease Middle School example, students were highly motivated to do work that was thorough and accurate because they needed to take their analysis to the principal as well as share with others around the United States and the world. They were motivated to understand how others thought about their work. Other features that would motivate students from the Pease example include working with peers, working with real-world equipment and tasks, and the capacity to communicate with experts locally and globally.

Functional

PBL is closely aligned with the needs of the 21st century because problems and projects are designed to simulate real-world contexts or actually involve students in real-world situations and conversations, preparing them with skills required for work in a rapidly changing global economy. Thus, PBL narrows the gap between school and work for jobs that require problem solving and reflection in action, technology, communication and presentation skills, leadership and teamwork roles, and greater ability to deal with interpersonal problems that arise in group work. These and other competencies, skills, and personal qualities are described in detail in the U.S. Departments of Labor and Education's document, *A Blueprint for High Performance: A SCANS Report for America 2000* (1992). PBL is, therefore, a good choice for schools wishing to align their instruction with skills needed for work.

There were many features of the Pease Middle School program that made student tasks and assessment authentic. Students used replicas of equipment used by experts, they performed a valuable community service, and they had various authentic audiences for their work. Moreover, they were guided to understand more complex cause-effect relationships. In other examples of problem-based learning, students become local experts on energy and other environmental issues; they have access to deep information about careers and community activities; and their work may be used by local communities and experts to solve problems of scientific inquiry. In one such case, student work was used by a local newspaper to report community responses to a nuclear reactor.

These examples show how community service or service learning is a natural methodology for problem-based learning. Service learning is currently spearheaded by two centers—Community Service Learning Center in Springfield, Massachusetts, and Project Service Leadership in Vancouver, Washington—and various service learning agencies across the United States. Kinsley and McPherson (1995) from these two centers respectively, have developed a major resource book for people interested in learning about the topic. Although the hope is that service learning projects involve challenging problems, not all of them do. If service learning projects focus on ill-structured or open-ended problems, however, the work is very motivational because it is valued by the local community. In these problem-based, service learning projects, students typically learn through active participation in well-organized service experiences. Ideally such experiences are developed collaboratively with school and community; provide structured time for the student to reflect, think, talk, and write about the experiences; provide opportunities to apply academic skills; and help foster the sense of caring for others.

In earlier times, most learning experiences occurred within the context of the home, community, or workplace in informal learning and in apprenticeships. This made the work authentic because there was an audience who cared, and this motivated children to learn. Family and community members were powerful role models who made the children feel that their work was valued. With the growth of schools as we know them today, these connections were lost.

Abbott (1995) argued that what is needed is to reconnect schools and communities. In part this assertion is about reconnecting children to the life and work of the community. Children should be given the chance to address local issues such as care for the elderly, programming for local television, and water quality analysis. Communities need children who can participate in local and state government. However, this reconnection is also about changing the relationship between schooling and policy. Today, schools often perceive the role of government in education as adversarial, and many policymakers have lost faith in schools as a viable public institution. Service learning is an opportunity for schools to involve local community members, business partners, and policymakers in discussions about the needs of the community and in celebration of children's services to the community.

In the Pease Middle School example, the students were performing a service to their school: measuring the quality of the air, which has implications for the health of the students. In Goal 7, the Profile developed by the Illinois

Mathematics and Science Academy also involves service learning concepts.

To summarize, various strands of research from cognitive sciences support the use of problem-based learning. PBL facilitates comprehension and memory. It is consistent with the new thinking in science, brain-based research, research on multiple intelligences, and constructivism. Students are motivated to learn in problem-based projects because (a) the skills and knowledge are aligned with real-world tasks or the needs of the local community; (b) interactions with other students, community members, and experts are usually challenging and exciting; and (c) involving students in problem formulation, self-assessments, generation of representation of the work, and debriefings gives them ownership. Finally, communities need problem-based learning because its methods and outcomes are well aligned to local needs as well as needs of the 21st century.

DIFFERENCES AMONG PROBLEM-BASED LEARNING APPROACHES

There are many different models of problem-based learning; however, it is beyond the scope of this book to review them all. The ones we have chosen to review below are among the more predominant. Further, we distributed research on each of these models throughout the Profiles that were developed by the author teams.

Medical Models of PBL

The idea of problem-based learning has spread not only throughout the medical professions but also throughout health-related professions generally. It is appropriate to begin with the two medical models of PBL that were developed for use with medical students at McMasters University in Canada by Woods and by Barrows, the fathers of PBL on this side of the Atlantic.

Barrows and his colleagues (1986) developed a tutorial model of PBL to help interns apply large quantities of information within the context of a simulation of the real problem: What is the diagnosis? They felt that diagnostic information, traditionally memorized for a test, would be more effectively used in later real-life situations once mastered through such problem-based learning. Someone is trained to play the role of a patient with a particular problem. The model includes developing a database from a huge battery of test data for the simulated patient, providing a facilitator who generally plays the role of Socratic questioner, and designing a performance-based assessment that requires students to interview the patient and relevant family to deal with the diagnosis. In recent years, Barrows has worked in the United States, first with the Illinois Mathematics and Science Academy (see Profile in Goal 7), then with a national network of high schools emphasizing medical careers for minorities. (See also Goal 5, where Rasmussen talks further about Barrow's notion of an ill-structured or ill-defined, open-ended problem.)

Woods developed his version of PBL for medical students enrolled in chemical engineering classes at McMasters. He was concerned that after spending so many years focusing on individual competition and memorizing information in textbooks, many students lack the social and emotional skills to cope with feelings encountered when learning the "new" PBL approach, negotiate and carry out a collaborative work plan, and self-assess progress (personal communication, April 1994). His model begins by asking participants to consider their readiness for change and to recognize the "grieving" process for coping with change. Considerable attention was given to developing both social skills and skills for independent learning before engaging in a PBL seminar. Some of the McMasters Problem Solving Units he developed include coping with conflict, basics of interpersonal skills, time management, decision making, and chairperson skills. Woods' books (1994; 1995) are packed with practical advice appropriate for anyone beginning PBL.

Cognitive Apprenticeship and Communities of Practice

Much of the work in this book was spearheaded by the parallel work of cognitive scientists who argued that learning is maximized if student work is situated in real-life contexts (e.g., Collins, Brown, & Holum, 1991). In such contexts, the work centers around real-world problems and performance-based assessments with authentic audiences. The concept of cognitive apprenticeship was used to capture the essence of the new role and relationship between teacher and student that must take place when learning is situated in authentic contexts. That is, teachers would no longer be information givers with students acting as passive recipients of knowledge. Instead, teachers would be coaches and mentors, and students would be cognitive apprentices who learn concepts and academic skills from teachers in much the same ways that apprentices learn from masters in the crafts.

Although authenticity and new roles characterize problem-based learning, much of the work in PBL is defined by the social interactions of *communities of practice*. According to Wenger (1995), communities of practice are different from teams, groups, work units, and networks. It is engagement in the practice, not proximity, or similarity of work or function that defines the community. This is in part because the norms that emerge from common goals and shared work and from sustained interactions over time hold the community together. According to Wenger,

> We don't just live to do things mechanically, but also and perhaps foremost, to participate, to belong in specific ways through our engagement in practices. Indeed, it is in our belonging that we find identities as human beings and that we are thus able to experience the world and our lives as meaningful. (1995, p. 18)

Such communities of practice can be developed in any context in school with or without technology, although networked technologies are a great help in building and sustaining collaborative work.

Research-Based Technology Projects

The diverse uses of technology in schools include anything from programmed learning to artificial intelligence to networked projects linking students to databases and experts through the Internet. Generally, researchers with technology-rich classrooms assume that technology is a tool to achieve both academic and social goals (communication and collaboration). Research-based technology projects typically involve some variation of problem-based learning. TERC in Boston, for example, has developed the concept of project-enhanced science learning, or PESL, which is described more fully in the Profile from Gladstone school in Goal 5.

A second example of PBL in which technology is used comes from the Cognition and Technology Group at Vanderbilt (1992). In their philosophy of anchored instruction, complex and interesting problems are presented in video narratives in which data have been embedded. Students constantly refer back to the video to retrieve bits of information as needed. Thus, the narrative is the conceptual anchor for the problem and sustained inquiry. Students work in groups to solve the problems in different ways.

A third example of a technology-rich approach to learning is the Cooperative Networked Educational Community of Tomorrow (CO-NECT). Each school in the CO-NECT project develops its own application of core principles, such as providing students with authentic, interdisciplinary tasks and problems. In one CO-NECT school, the school year is divided into four 9-week cycles, each with a different global theme. Students and teachers develop a class project collaboratively for each cycle. Some CO-NECT schools engage in sustained inquiry in conjunction with worldwide scientific expeditions such as EARTHWATCH's Mystery of the Pipe Wreck project in the Caribbean. In investigations like this, students and teachers can often download data from project sites, engage in data analysis, and communicate electronically with past project participants and current project staff (Bolt, Beraneck, & Newman, Inc., 1993).

One Co-nect student, after an Internet search of more than 200 addresses, e-mailed a lawyer in Northern Ireland to ask for information on a research question: Can there be lasting peace in Northern Ireland? The lawyer replied with a two-page e-mail letter with current news and perspectives on this issue. Although the unit described in the Profile from Abbott Middle School in Goal 4 is not part of the Co-nect project, the students and teachers plan to use technology as a tool in similar ways; in this case, to make a proposal for a public sculpture in the local community.

Research on Expertise

In the book, *Surpassing Ourselves,* Berieter and Scardamalia (1993) argue that expertise is a process of progressive problem solving in which people continuously rethink and redefine their tasks. Progressive problem solving for experts becomes a disposition in which there is a need to continually surpass their own performance, to make an original contribution, and to do better. Developing expertise in students involves, among other things, a process of continually making knowledge public. This cultivates expertise by making thinking explicit, testing ideas against multiple perspectives and different situations or conditions, enabling people to help each other, sharing objectives and resources. This act of making knowledge public is very different from current models of schooling. Indeed, Bereiter and Scardamalia argue that schools lack most of the conditions that produce expertise; this deficit, they say, is a major problem for America.

To define conditions for the classroom, Bereiter and Scardamalia apply the conditions of scientific research and development (R&D), which focus heavily on writing for scientific journals. When publishing their work, scientists make their knowledge and thinking public and demonstrate both individual contributions and contributions to the collective goals of the community; that is, knowledge building. Students in the classroom would therefore benefit from sustained inquiry, a focus on problems rather than categories of knowledge, progressive problem solving, and an emphasis on collective (group and classroom) goals. Regarding the latter, the authors believe that assessment of students should be based at least in part on their contributions to the advancement of the collective knowledge rather than solely on individual attainment. In Bereiter and Scardamalia's design, teachers focus on ways to make student theories and hypotheses public through various processes, especially producing and explaining their own theories and hypotheses.

Bereiter and Scardamalia developed a powerful computer-assisted learning environment called Computer Supported Intentional Learning Environments (CSILE; in press) to apply these ideas in Canada and the United States. Regrettably, neither csile nor its commercial version, Co-Learning, are readily available.

PBL for Educators

Although, there is no basic research book on PBL for all educators, Bridges and Hallinger (1992) have written a classic book for administrators that teachers will find helpful. In this book the authors distinguish three types of instruction:

1. Traditional instruction.

2. Case-based studies that we would classify as something between PBL and text-based interdisciplinary instruction; although these studies focused on questions related to the cases (a PBL quality), the questions and issues were largely defined by the teacher.

3. PBL, which they define in terms of five characteristics.
    (a) The starting point for learning is a problem.
    (b) The problem is one that administrators in training are apt to face as future professionals.

(c) The knowledge that they are expected to acquire during their professional training is organized around problems rather than the disciplines.

(d) Administrator students, individually and collectively, assume the major responsibility for their own instruction and learning.

(e) Most of the learning occurs in small groups rather than lectures. (p.6)

Clearly, this model for adult learners is very similar to the characteristics we have discussed for PBL for younger students, and was in fact heavily influenced by Barrows' work. Bridges and Hallinger also distinguish between problem-stimulated learning, in which students work in teams to address specific problems, and student-centered learning. With problem-stimulated learning, the problems, objectives, materials, and resources are defined largely, if not entirely, by the teacher. The Profile developed by IMSA on garbage illustrates this approach to PBL. Student-centered learning emphasizes the goal of fostering the skills needed for lifelong learning. To address this goal, the instructor may present the problem as is typical in the workplace, but students identify learning issues they wish to explore and proceed to locate the materials and resources that pertain to their self-defined issues.

PBL as Codevelopment

Although we define our model of PBL-CD in subsequent chapters, we feel it would be helpful to provide an overview here to place it in the context of the other models of PBL described above. Our model is based on the belief that people build expertise in problem-based teaching and learning by engaging in progressive problem solving. Specifically, we have designed the process as a series of cycles of making knowledge explicit and refining the thinking. Our basic cycle repeats four fundamental thinking processes: (a) understanding and planning, (b) acting and sharing,

Progressive Problem—Solving To Build Expertise

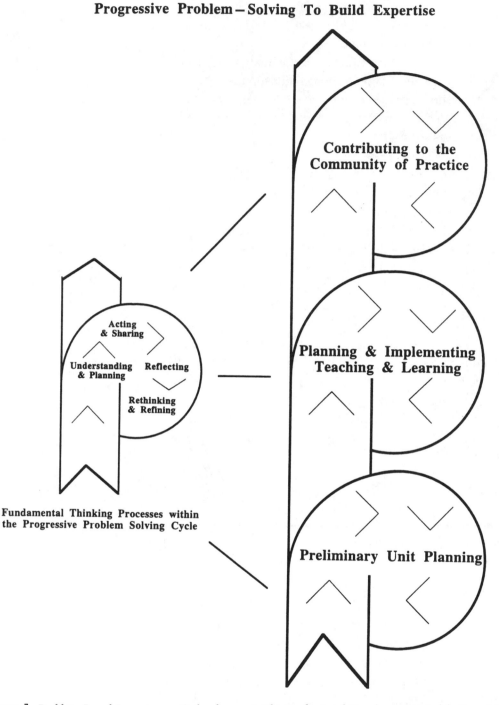

Figure 1 *Problem-Based Learning as Codevelopment: The Professional Development Model. Copyright B. Jones, C. Rasmussen, and M. Moffitt. (1995). North Central Regional Educational Laboratory, Oak Brook, IL. Used by permission.*

(c) reflecting, and (d) rethinking and revision. This cycle is shown in the small spiral in Figure 1.

As illustrated, teachers engage in progressive problem solving in three major stages of our Professional Development Model: (a) during preliminary unit planning, (b) when planning and implementing teaching and learning in the classroom, and (c) when refining a PBL unit for the purpose of contributing to a community of practice.

Teachers and students also use the progressive problem solving cycle throughout their teaching and learning in the classroom when (a) identifying specific problems, (b) developing a plan of inquiry or work, (c) conducting the inquiry and analysis, (d) preparing and presenting the findings from the inquiry, and (e) debriefing and consolidation.

As an example, while planning and implementing a PBL unit in the classroom, teachers use progressive problem solving to build their expertise about teaching and learning. They engage in the equivalent of lesson planning for the ways in which the five phases of problem solving would play out in the classroom; share their plans with us or their colleagues; teach the unit, maybe even while being observed by a critical friend; reflect on their practice; rethink and revise on the basis of the experience including debriefing with us or their colleagues; and, when possible, reteach the unit improving upon it.

PBL-CD has many similarities to the models described earlier, and in some ways it represents a synthesis of elements of those models. That is, it has elements of expertise building, progressive problem solving, communities of practice, authentic contexts, and open-ended problems. Moreover, because we encourage teachers to apply research on learning and teaching to their unit development, many of our teachers choose research on multiple intelligences, the brain, collaborative learning, or service learning.

PBL-CD is unique in applying knowledge building and progressive problem solving as the focus for working with teachers and other educators in authentic tasks. That is, we work with teachers first on an authentic, problem-based task of curriculum development so that they can fully experience the codevelopment, progressive problem solving, and critical friend process before they teach it to students. Each of these features will be discussed more fully in Goals 2 and 3.

P̱ʙʟ-ᴄᴅ emphasizes codevelopment in many ways: (a) between professional developers and teachers; (b) among teachers; (c) between teachers and students; and (d) among teachers, students, and the broader research and development community. The breadth and depth of codevelopment further distinguishes our model.

Finally, whereas Bereiter and Scardamalia developed their progressive problem solving primarily for students using technology, we have developed our model for teachers and students with or without technology.

SOME PRACTICAL ADVICE FOR IMPLEMENTING INTERDISCIPLINARY, PROBLEM-BASED UNITS

Before we provide more detail about the key features of our model in the next chapter, we want to share some research that gives sound, practical advice on implementing interdisciplinary, problem-based learning. First, Roth and others caution to start small with a unit developed by one teacher or a small group over a relatively short period of time, such as 2 to 6 weeks (cited in Willis, 1995, p. 3). It is hard to devote adequate attention to designing powerful learning opportunities for a semester or year-long unit if it is the first time the teacher is responsible for collaborative skills, alternative scheduling, teaming, or providing diverse resources.

Second, Roth (in Willis, 1994) argues that "thematic units often fail to focus on powerful ideas or organizing concepts from the disciplines" (p. 3) because teachers often select concepts to go with the theme rather than focus on what students need and want to learn. Thus, important content may not be well integrated or may even be overlooked. Moreover, in multidisciplinary approaches it is easy for one discipline to overshadow another. One good strategy for addressing these problems is to begin with a good concept map of essential material to cover in each subject area. Then teachers can frequently refer back to the map and develop ways to involve students in learning opportunities that focus on those concepts. In Goal 5 the Profile developed by Edison to create a museum display on parallel evolution was mapped in this way. Another strategy is to pay close attention to national, state, and local standards and benchmarks within each subject. Several of the Profiles in this book involved working back and forth between the standards and content.

Third, it is vital to honor students' interests (Krogh, cited in Willis, 1995, p. 3) as well as their culture and past experiences. This is important for learning as well as for self-esteem and motivation. We need to take individuals and groups of students where they are and develop various social and interpersonal skills, recognizing that each group of students will be different in its social and cognitive abilities as well as interests. Although many of the Profiles in this book attend to these issues, they are a major focus in the two Profiles in Goal 4 on cross-cultural projects.

Fourth, various strategies exist for team teaching, scheduling planning meetings, and unit organization. Jacobs (1989) presents teachers with options as simple as having two teachers organize or "correlate" the subject matter in their individual courses to support and reinforce the other. For example, if a social studies teacher focuses on problems related to the internment of Japanese Americans during World War II, the English teacher's literature course could be sequenced to provide various types of prose written by internees. More complex units beg for common planning time and scheduling sustained periods of study. Kasak (in Jones, Rasmussen, & Moffitt, 1996) stresses that the following time-related elements need to be put in place:

◻ Common team planning in excess of four times a week in addition to the teacher's individual preparation time.

◻ Duration of common planning time equal to 40 minutes a day.

❑ Smaller teacher-student ratios on each interdisciplinary team, with optimal team size under 120 students for 5 to 7 teachers.

❑ Time for teams to improve their performance as a team.

Finally, Blumenfeld and her colleagues (1991) indicate that PBL and its predecessor, learning by doing, had very good results but the results were not as widespread as desired. They believe that this is largely because projects were advanced and disseminated without adequate appreciation of the teacher knowledge and skills needed to implement them effectively. Among other things, it was not well understood how much knowledge was required to motivate and engage students in challenging tasks, how to consider questions from the point of view of the student, how to manage the complexity of the classroom, or how to prepare students for participation in projects.

At the same time, the authors argue that the design of problem-focused projects can address these issues. For example, student interest and the perceived value of the lesson will be enhanced when (a) tasks are varied and include novel elements, (b) the problem is authentic and challenging, (c) artifacts are created providing closure and evidence of participation, (d) there is choice about what or how the work is done, and (e) there are opportunities to work with others.

Our model, PBL-CD, has features that address each of these design issues. In the next Goal we discuss those features and some of the ways in which students, teachers, administrators, and support staff have responded to problem-based teaching and learning and the professional development of such practices.

1 **Understanding and Planning**: In the self-directed activities following the Introduction you identified one or more practices that you were "truly ready to change." Identify the ways in which research and best practice support your changes and stimulate further planning. Think about the cognitive, motivational, and functional grounds for PBL, as well as the Pease Middle School example and the various approaches to PBL discussed in this goal.

What practices are you ready to change?	In what ways does the research on learning support this change?

Given the practical advice offered in this goal, what ideas do you have for your next steps?

2 **Acting and Sharing**: Select one or more of the practices you have identified above and try them in your classroom. Share your experiences with one or more critical friends. Describe your plans for your informal conference below.
The process for a critical friend dialogue should include

☐ sharing your desired outcome for the conversation
☐ asking your critical friend to practice active listening and ask clarifying questions
☐ asking your critical friend to offer constructive, nonjudgmental feedback

3 **Reflecting**: Reflect upon your experiences in trying out and sharing your interdisciplinary problem-based practices. List or in some way represent them (metaphor, graphic organizer, icon).

4 **Rethinking and Refining**: What are the implications of this for further refining your practice?

goal 2

What Is Problem-Based Learning as Codevelopment and What Are the Benefits?

In Goal 1 we made the case for problem-based learning (PBL) in general, and for our model of Problem-Based Learning as Codevelopment (PBL-CD) in particular, sharing evidence from research and best practice. Now we want to describe specific features of PBL-CD, many of which you'll recognize in the research- and field-based examples throughout this book and in the practice of educators like Bill and Carmen.

There are eight key features of Problem-Based Learning as Codevelopment (see Figure 2).

1. As do all models of problem-based learning, PBL-CD addresses complex issues and open-ended questions or prob-

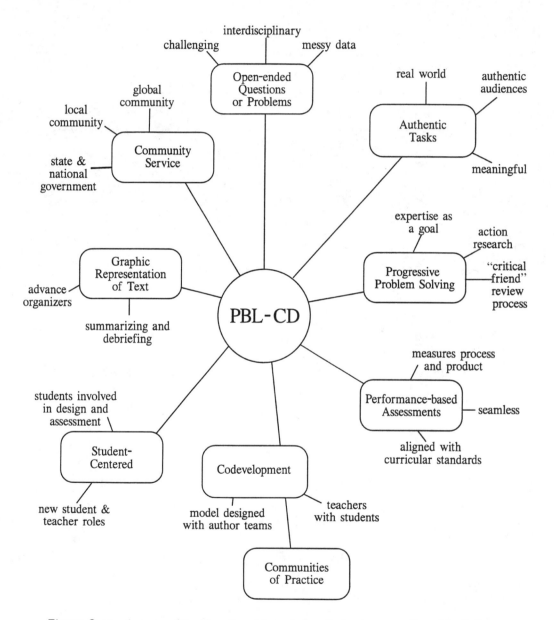

Figure 2 *Key features of Problem-Based Learning as Codevelopment. Copyright B. Jones, C. Rasmussen, and M. Moffitt, (1995). North Central Regional Educational Laboratory, Oak Brook, IL. Used by permission.*

lems. Open-ended questions, often referred to as ill-structured problems, are innately challenging in part because there is no single correct response or simple answer. These questions often involve messy data that may be incomplete, inconsistent, or ambiguous. In addition, each question has multiple perspectives and is broad enough to involve multiple disciplines. And even though students have a limited amount of time to find answers, open-ended questions stimulate students to look into various resources and modes of inquiry.

2. In the PBL-CD model, it is important that learning takes place within the context of authentic tasks. This principle is common to all constructivist approaches including problem-based learning. In these approaches, tasks, issues, and problems for students are aligned with the tasks, issues, and problems in the real world—including all their complexities, messy data, multiple perspectives, and potential solutions. This is one aspect that makes them authentic. Another aspect is the audience. The question we always ask in examining or creating an authentic task is, Who cares? If the teacher and student care only for the purposes of a grade, it is not authentic. Authentic tasks and performances necessarily involve contexts and audiences that are meaningful to the student such as local community members and parents, experts, the broader business community, and policymakers. Such audiences make the work valued in a culturally important social context.

3. Another feature of our model is that students and teachers engage in progressive problem solving. Although other models of problem-based learning incorporate problem solving, this feature in our model was adapted from Bereiter and Scardamalia's (1993) concept of progressive problem solving for students discussed in Goal 1. Progressive problem solving, as we use it, incorporates four fundamental thinking processes: (a) understanding and planning, (b) acting and sharing, (c) reflecting, and (d) rethinking and refining. Teachers and students engage in this progressive problem solving cycle throughout investigations in the classroom and community. We also use this concept to develop learning environments for teams of

teachers and others who, in turn, develop teaching-learning approaches and share their research. We refer to these groups as author teams because they are developing their research in the classroom as curriculum studies.

❑ We urge author teams to focus on developing expertise as a goal for themselves: We ask teachers to develop expertise in their unit subject matter, skills, and instructional strategies by teaching the unit, or a variation of it, repeatedly.

❑ We want teams to understand that they are part of an educational R&D community that values expertise and applying research to teaching and learning. Specifically, we encourage teachers to engage in progressive action research so that they continually refine their theories of learning and teaching by conducting classroom research.

❑ To provide multiple perspectives, quality control, and self-reflection, we introduce critical friend review processes. We ask each team to take on the role of critical friends with one another in order to provide feedback in the form of clarifying questions, helpful critiques, and advocacy (Costa & Kallick, 1993).

❑ Finally, we use a Profile template as a set of flexible guidelines for author teams to refer to when describing the design and development of PBL units so that the broader learning community can discuss and build on the research, design, and experiences of each generation of teacher teams.

4. In PBL-CD authentic tasks and problem-based inquiry necessitate performance-based assessments. Presentations of authentic work can not be adequately measured only by traditional tests. Assessment that measures both the process and the final products of an investigation provides more information about progress, about what has been learned, and the ways in which leaning is meaningful. Assessment that takes place throughout the PBL process is also more likely to be seamless—that is, a more natural and well-in-

tegrated part of instruction. We have found that it is particularly important to align performance-based assessments with curricular standards and benchmarks.

5. A major goal of our model is to engage teachers, students, and others in a codevelopment process as members of communities of practice. PBL-CD involves codevelopment in several ways: among teachers; between teachers and students; and among teachers, students, and the broader community. First, we want teachers to experience the codevelopment process as authors engaged in the authentic task of creating PBL curricula and sharing them with colleagues within their school communities. This book, in fact, represents an authentic product that extends that sharing to a broader community of practice. Although the members of our PBL-CD community of practice may not have known each other well or related in other contexts, problem-based learning provided the structure to our relationships and allowed the common work to advance. Second, codevelopment means that teachers consult students about the problems, issues, and questions of interest to them; about what goals, experiments, and inquiry methods they think are most appropriate to address their problems; about what assessments and criteria are appropriate for quality work; and about other aspects of the work. Therefore, the role of the teacher is that of coinvestigator, codeveloper, and colearner, not giver of information. The teacher and students are members of a community of practice that, in many cases, extends well beyond them and their classroom walls.

6. As with most constructivist and problem-based models, in PBL-CD the teaching-learning process is student-centered in specific ways. When teachers involve students in defining the tasks, problems, and issues, the students will have greater ownership for learning and they will be highly motivated to work through an inquiry process (Blumenfeld et al., 1991). This feature of PBL can be very challenging for many teachers. It is not easy to anticipate student-generated tasks and problems and, at the same time, link them to the array of curriculum objectives, learner outcomes, and

required assessments. Yet when both students and teachers move toward expanded roles of colearners, coinvestigators, coproducers, and coevaluators, learning becomes more engaging for all.

7. As with many constructivist instructional approaches, our model involves an emphasis on using graphic representations of text (or organizational patterns as they are sometimes called) at various points in the PBL-CD process (Jones, Pierce, & Hunter, 1988). These include graphs such as tables, flow charts, Venn diagrams, cycles, and concept maps as well as the traditional semantic webs. The graphs and organizational patterns serve different purposes throughout the teaching and learning processes. Examples of their use are integrated into the illustration offered in Appendix C.

8. Finally, we encourage author teams to consider the element of community service discussed in Goal 1. This is in part because we want to help reconnect schools to the local community, the business community, higher education, and policymakers. Tasks that involve services for the community make the work and its assessment more meaningful. Moreover, working with the community provides multiple perspectives and authentic audiences.

IMPACT ON MEMBERS OF THE COMMUNITY

The transformation from other approaches to problem-based learning differs for groups in both benefits to be gained and issues to be resolved, including the issue of readiness. Teachers like Bill and Carmen, who already have some of the values and skills needed for this approach, may find the process of change relatively easy (and both scary and exciting). However, for educators, students, and others who need a lot of structure, quiet, predictability, and adherence to rules, this approach may not initially be too appealing. In this section, we discuss the benefits and implementation issues for the various groups involved in change: students, teachers, principals, district staff, librarians, media specialists, and technology providers.

Students

We saw in Goal 1 that PBL students are generally more highly motivated, have deeper and more lasting comprehension, are better problem solvers, and have better communication and collaboration skills. There is also much in the literature on PBL about the growth that takes place when students take on new collaborative roles such as leader, synthesizer, critical friend, evaluator, and planner as well as various team roles. As teachers become more collaborative, students feel freer to formulate their own questions, define problems (including ones they have in the classroom), help others spontaneously, and solve problems on their own.

What teachers report to us and what we observe about students who use PBL-CD is the sense of community and shared responsibility that develops in the classroom if learning outcomes and assessments are codeveloped and if students regularly use critical friend processes. Moreover, teachers and principals in our project frequently comment about how much more powerful it is when presentations and assessments are public and the students have the opportunity to debrief, a process incorporated into many PBL models but often left out by researchers and teachers.

One potential negative effect sometimes noted in PBL classrooms is that high-achieving students who are used to getting good grades based on their ability to learn isolated facts and skills sometimes experience anxiety as PBL is introduced into the classroom. Typically, such students are used to having the right answers and having both teachers and other students look to them for leadership and for setting the standards. In PBL activities, initially they may feel that they no longer have that edge. These students go through a period of adjustment as they learn to respect the opinions and abilities of others. This problem typically diminishes though as they learn how PBL and collaborative processes work and how empowering it is to codevelop problems and a plan of work with students in other schools, teachers, and other adults.

Another concern is that, as with any type of cooperative learning, some students may be willing to allow the more active and high-achieving students to do all the work, or more than their share of the work. This is why it is important for teachers to provide ways to assess individual work as well as group work. The reality is that such students are often less active in the classroom anyway, but in a collaborative or cooperative context, there is the issue of fairness to the rest of the group as well. Working in such groups can be a stimulus to engage these less active students in interaction with peers and self-assessment to reflect on their behavior and develop new standards and commitments to learning.

In the final analysis, we believe that interdisciplinary PBL units can have very dramatic results for students. The Profiles in Goals 4 through 7 provide examples of students engaged enthusiastically in very challenging tasks.

Teachers

Because problem-based learning is typically interdisciplinary, some of the teacher responses arise from the experience of cross-disciplinary teaming. Teaching in teams necessarily takes teachers out of isolated classrooms, allowing much greater opportunity to discuss the past experiences, culture, and needs of individual students and to work together to meet student needs.

A statewide survey of middle and high schools implementing such approaches reveals that most teachers also experience greater satisfaction and appreciate the level of support provided to them by their teams (Kasak, in Jones, Rasmussen & Moffitt, 1996). The Carnegie Corporation report (1989), *Turning Points: Preparing American Youth for the 21st Century,* was a major catalyst in the movement toward team teaching with its recommendation to create small communities for learning.

Kasak's review of the literature on teaming found four broad areas of team functioning: curriculum coordination;

coordination of student assignments, assessments, and feedback; parental contact and involvement, and contact with other building resource staff. Each of these areas has particular activities and areas of mutual support associated with it. For example, the area of curriculum coordination includes:

❑ Setting goals and objectives related to student learning

❑ Planning special team projects and activities

❑ Developing community learning opportunities and activities for students working together

❑ Integrating, coordinating, and evaluating curricula across subject areas

❑ Using block scheduling to achieve instructional goals

Other teacher responses to problem-based learning relate to the shift from reliance on textbooks to student-generated data and materials, the use of technology, and deployment of others outside the school as teachers, role models, and experts. The following e-mail from Kim Alamar at Whittier Elementary School reflects a response that we see quite often: an enthusiasm that is sometimes exhausting but always exciting.

> Kids brainstormed ideas like creating a video, radio announcements, etc. We decided/guided them to publish a newspaper. Using the questions, the kids broke into research groups by secret ballot, created group behavior rubrics, and then dove into research via fax, Internet interviews, and books. It was truly exciting and draining. There were times when students were in four different areas of the building. As a teacher, that is one of the most difficult, no control-type of feelings. We survived and had terrific responses from

scientists and experts from all over the USA. (personal communication, November 1995)

This methodology and Kim's work in general represent a major leap forward in understanding and implementing PBL-CD.

Many teachers new to PBL ask about developing the competencies students need for inquiry and self-regulated learning (Blumenfeld et al., 1991). Students need to have sufficient knowledge of content and skills to raise interesting questions and conduct research. Also, it is desirable that they also have some proficiency at using technology as tools for their research. Finally, they need strong cognitive and metacognitive skills to generate plans, systematically make and test predictions, interpret evidence, and come up with good solutions. While this is a challenge for some teachers, the reality is that PBL tasks and thinking processes engage students' interest so thoroughly that such competencies develop more rapidly than expected in most instances.

Another interest and role that teachers are often ready to contemplate is how to involve local community members as resources for learning and audiences for public presentation or performances. We have been amazed at the creative, energetic, and successful ways that teachers have involved students in the community. One class conducted research on a nuclear reactor that would be located near them. Part of their research involved communicating their results to the local press and to local policymakers. One of the teacher-authored profiles in this book involves students building a display for the local children's museum; other profiles involve addressing a local health problem, a proposal for a public sculpture that students submit to the City Council, and the problem of garbage within the community. There are many wonderful and often powerful rewards for connecting students to local and global communities. These new learning opportunities encourage teachers to be entrepreneurs, expanding their students and their own interests and horizons.

Principals and District Staff

Researchers recognize that problem-focused, learning-centered approaches need more time and flexible scheduling than is allotted in the typical school (e.g., R. Jones, 1995; Schoenstein, 1995). Indeed, Kasak (in Jones, Rasmussen, & Moffitt, 1996) concludes that because it takes time to develop units and teacher expertise and comfort, administrators and district support must be present to establish a school-within-a-school program. They must be willing to create opportunities for teachers to take risks and for acceptance of innovation. We agree with Kasak that it is vital that principals and district staff provide adequate time for teachers to develop PBL units (see Goal 1). We affirm the importance of supporting a school climate for calculated risk-taking and sound experimentation. We have found that it is possible to create successful problem-based approaches to interdisciplinary teaching and learning without creating a school-within-a-school in formal ways. For example, at Whittier Elementary, the principal was working toward involving all teachers in at least two PBL units per year. In the Edison Profile in Goal 4, the principal wanted to launch a single, powerful pilot unit involving multiple grade levels for a number of weeks. In other instances, the whole school may be involved in a large-scale PBL project such as building a space shuttle simulation or solving a community problem.

Principals and schools benefit from becoming involved in the development of units. Through their involvement they can assure that the subject areas are balanced and well integrated, not just correlated or integrated superficially. It is very easy for one subject area to dominate (Willis, 1994); however, the principal can seek a good alignment of objectives within and between subjects and grades. There is also the question of balance between encouraging teachers to take risks, and meeting certain local and state objectives. Participating in performance-based assessments and their debriefing would be a valuable experience for principals wherever this is possible. Assuming a greater role in PBL unit development will likely involve principals and district staff in more collaborative team conferences rather than in more directive approaches.

For our own work, the story of two elementary principals from very different schools is noteworthy. Sheila Schlagger, principal of Edison Regional Gifted Center, and Irene DaMota, principal of Whittier Elementary, had never met before this project. However, as a result of our PBL-CD community of practice, they collaborated to write a grant proposal to provide "practitioners' collaboratories" in their schools and four others. This concept and the proposal writing process they undertook, embodies the very best in community of practice and codevelopment concepts. In this grant, which they won, teachers from each school will visit and learn from the teachers at the other school, collaborating to develop problem-based units. Teachers and principals at both schools will also work to develop assessment strategies that demonstrate both the talents of the teachers and the abilities of the students in ways that community members and policymakers can accept.

Librarians, Media Specialists, and Technology Providers

In the past, the roles of librarians, media specialists, and technology providers were typically support roles at best. As interdisciplinary and problem-based learning have flourished, persons in these roles have often had the opportunity to become leaders within schools, districts and states, and the country (Jones, Valdez, Nowakowski, & Rasmussen, 1994).

Sometimes the roles of this leadership have been working with teachers and principals to design units. These roles are illustrated both in the parallel evolution unit developed by the librarian and media specialist at Edison (in Goal 5) and in the sculpture unit developed by a Waukegan middle school teacher, Ted Injasulian, with the support of the district middle school technology coordinator, Jo Williamson (see Goal 4). In Waukegan, the high school library media specialist, Jane Yoder, provides support to local teachers in curriculum writing and extends her leadership role to state professional organizations.

Sometimes this leadership has focused on implementing problem-based learning opportunities throughout a state or on the Internet. (See Profile about the Discovery Channel Internet site developed by Will Duggan and Andree Duggan in Goal 7.) We feel that these changing roles are long overdue and will benefit students and teachers where these new support roles emerge.

Professional Development Specialists and Researchers

The shift from teaching to learning and the parallel shift from learning as individuals to learning in teams and groups involved in codevelopment has profound consequences for the beliefs and behavior for professional development specialists and researchers. Some have wanted to take small, careful steps, being cautious to maintain the quality of the instruction. Others boldly embrace and create new ideas, forge new paths, and anticipate a new era with greatly expanded roles for adults and children. Yet however cautious or grand the ambition, clearly the journey is as important as the products, and that journey can be very exciting. We have already described in the Preface how powerful these shifts have been in our lives. We are pleased also to learn of other professional development and research groups moving more toward involving teachers and others in problem-based learning and codevelopment experiences. The Illinois Mathematics and Science Academy Profile in Goal 7 is an example.

Now that you have an understanding of the key features of PBL-CD and their impact, in the next chapter we want to resume our journey, charting a path, step by step through our model of interdisciplinary, problem-based learning.

1 **Understanding and Planning**: Select a unit of study which you would like to make more interdisciplinary and problem-based. Use the features of Problem-Based Learning as Codevelopment (PBL-CD) to analyze and further develop your unit.

Features of PBL-CD	Description of current unit:	Plans for making this unit more interdisciplinary and problem-based:
Open-ended questions/ problems		
Authentic tasks		
Progressive problem-solving		
Performance-based assessments		
Codevelopment		
Student roles		
Teacher roles		

Graphical representations		
Community service		

---

2 **Acting and Sharing**: Share your analysis and plans for further development of your unit with a critical friend or friends. Talk about the potential impact of these changes on students, colleagues, parents, and others in the school community. Describe your plans for your informal conference below.

The process for a critical friend dialogue should include

☐ sharing your desired outcome for the conversation
☐ asking your critical friend to practice active listening and ask clarifying questions
☐ asking your critical friend to offer constructive, nonjudgmental feedback

3 | **Reflecting**: Reflect upon the analysis and plans shared with and by your critical friend(s). List or in some way represent them (metaphor, graphic organizer, icon).

4 | **Rethinking and Refining**: What are the implications of this for further refining your unit?

goal 3

Planning and Implementing Problem-Based Learning as Codevelopment

The path we are about to follow, step by step, through PBL-CD will show you both the complexity and the richness inherent in this professional development and curriculum development model. Along the way, we will get reacquainted with our fictional teacher team of Bill, Carmen, Eric, and Coretta as they illustrate the process of planning a PBL unit and show us what PBL "looks" and "sounds" like in the classroom.

Much of the time used for creating a PBL unit should be put into planning. The Planning Flowchart in Figure 3, illustrates the major steps in preliminary planning for a PBL unit. The Flowchart is meant to guide a team of teachers in their up-front, behind-the-scenes planning, moving from general considerations to specific decisions, from generating a large pool of ideas to choosing and refining tasks and problems for investigation. It is a somewhat complex process. Yet careful consideration of each aspect in the preliminary planning stage is more likely to result in an integrated, well-aligned, defensible unit of study.

The question and answer format that follows represents many of the questions that teachers ask as they plan PBL curriculum and instruction. It seems a natural and "interactive" guide for reflective practitioners to use when walking through the planning process.

Where do we begin? How do we set the parameters for our PBL unit?

In order to choose the parameters for a PBL unit, a natural starting point for most teachers is the selection of disciplines for a PBL study. Often one subject area serves as the basis of study, with other disciplines being integrated into that area. That was certainly the case with many of the teacher-authored profiles in the chapters that follow. Sometimes multiple disciplines are more or less equally integrated (i.e., mathematics and science or the humanities). For the purposes of planning a PBL unit, it is necessary for you to choose two or more subject areas for interdisciplinary study.

Given the important role that local, state, and national standards play in many schools, standards that must be addressed as a part of school improvement or reform should be given early consideration. A consideration of standards up-front does not mean that PBL should be standards- or outcomes-driven. Instead, it sets the stage for a later purposeful integration of standards into the unit and is more likely to result in a well-aligned, defensible course of study.

PROBLEM-BASED LEARNING AS CODEVELOPMENT: PRELIMINARY PLANNING FLOWCHART

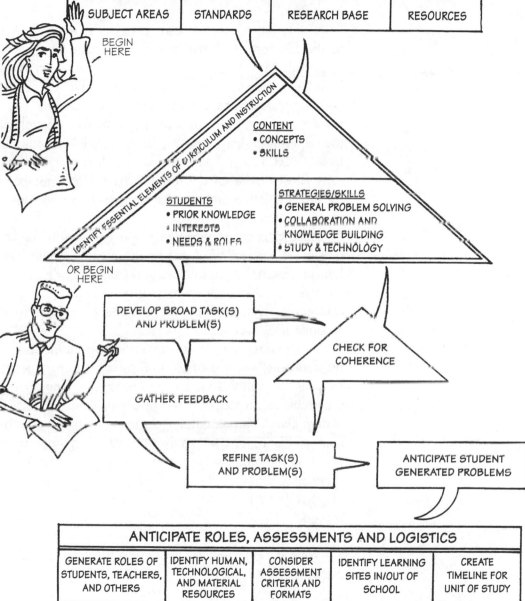

Figure 3 *Preliminary planning flowchart. Copyright B. Jones, C. Rasmussen, and M. Moffitt. (1995). North Central Regional Educational Laboratory, Oak Brook, IL. Used by permission.*

In addition, some of the professional standards and benchmarks, such as those in the Association for the Advancement of Science's Project 2061, identify big ideas and deep principles that can serve as meaningful sources of potential problems for the PBL unit and strengthen the curriculum overall.

The PBL-CD model has also brought the research base to the forefront. It is particularly important for a more open-ended investigation like problem-based learning to be well-grounded in both theory and best practice. So this is the optimal time to identify any research base that is especially important to your team. For example, a couple of the PBL Profiles that follow are based in part on multiple intelligences theory and practice (Gardner, 1993). This early consideration of the research base helped to shape the broad task and problem that became the guiding force in the PBL unit.

Another consideration that might help define the PBL unit is the availability of one or more exceptionally rich human, material, or technological resources. For example, an artist-in-residence, a school prairie or garden plot, a local community problem or program, or a technology-based program might serve as a catalyst for a unit.

By choosing the subject areas and considering possible standards, research bases, and resources as parameters for your PBL unit, you are likely to begin discussing possible problems. In fact, it is not uncommon for the choice of disciplines to prompt the suggestion of meaningful problems and questions for study—problems and questions based on important subject area concepts and principles. If potential problems do not emerge here, they will, in all likelihood, be a part of the next step in the planning process.

What other things should we consider before identifying the likely problem for study?

It is important to explore further and identify the essential elements of curriculum and instruction for each subject area and to make connections among them, beginning with content-specific concepts and skills. It may be helpful to begin by considering big ideas, concepts, and skills. This focus on each of the disciplines involved and their connections assures that content rather than pure interest, available resources, or fragments of content and skills becomes the primary "driver" of the PBL unit.

A second, equally important consideration is that of the students. In PBL there is a deliberate effort to build knowledge, beginning with the knowledge that students bring to the learning experience. Therefore, a discussion of students' prior knowledge and strengths is valuable at this point. It is also important to identify students' interests, especially as reflected in their cultural backgrounds and in issues of relevance to them. A practical, early consideration for many teachers is the range of special needs of their students. A discussion of needs can be helpful in identifying the potential roles of students in problem-based learning. Many teachers have found that behavior problems diminish during PBL and that previously unidentified strengths emerge during small group work. A discussion of your students' needs as well as their prior knowledge, strengths, and interests is likely to yield more promising planning.

Finally, it is beneficial to identify cross-curricular strategies and skills, including pertinent critical thinking and general problem-solving skills, social and cognitive skills needed for collaboration and knowledge building, study strategies, and technological skills.

It may be very helpful for you to brainstorm and display all of these elements so that connections are visible, and so that the lists can be revisited and added onto with further planning. We have known teams of teachers who have put these lists up on chart paper in the teacher workroom or lounge. This display enabled their colleagues to see at a glance how a single problem-based unit could incorporate multiple outcomes. It also encouraged the team to reflect continually on their planning.

These elements of curriculum and instruction, along with the standards identified in step 1, naturally lead to the "broad student outcomes" described in the PBL Profiles in subsequent chapters. They are instrumental in planning for well-integrated, defensible PBL units.

What problem do we really want students to investigate? How can we be sure that the task and problem are big enough and rich enough to address multiple goals?

While engaging in the brainstorming and analyzing described in step 2, meaningful topics and themes usually emerge, and it is possible to develop broad tasks and problems for study. The challenge of this step in the process is to go well beyond the identification of an interdisciplinary topic or theme to the articulation of one or more potential authentic tasks and problems. It is critical to keep the task and problem broad—big enough to allow for student-generated problems for later small group inquiry. If a task and problem are too narrowly defined, they will limit student codevelopment and ownership of the study. It may be helpful to you to pose the questions listed in Exhibit 1 to facilitate this sometimes difficult transition from meaningful topic to significant problem.

EXHIBIT 1	Questions for Transforming Study Topics Into Problems

In what ways are the task(s) and problem(s) worth knowing or significant to the lives of students and society?
How do the task and the problem . . .

❏ represent authentic, real world tasks?

❏ incorporate multiple goals?

❏ respond to student interests?

❏ encourage student-generated problems?

❏ lead to multiple tasks and investigative activities?

❏ encourage students to take action?

How can we be sure that our problem and task best represent our curriculum and instruction?

Once you have agreed upon a broad task and problem, it is beneficial to check for coherence between the task and problem and the elements of curriculum and instruction (from step 2). Perhaps there could be a better fit, or maybe something is missing and the task and problem suggest additional elements for integration.

Who can give us helpful feedback on our preliminary ideas?

It is also beneficial to test out your ideas and gather feedback from others, including other teachers, resource specialists, and administrators, as well as available experts-in-the-field. It can be very insightful to gather feedback on preliminary ideas from students and parents, too.

This is the first of several pivotal points in the PBL-CD professional development process where teams of teachers take on the role of "critical friends" with one another. Guidelines for engaging in the critical friend process, adapted from Costa and Kallick (Jones, Rasmussen, & Moffitt, 1996), follow:

□ Learner team sets desired outcomes for the conference. For example, the team may ask for specific types of feedback such as the appropriateness of the open-ended question or seek overall reactions. Learner team provides a "practice" (e.g., draft plan for a PBL unit or an observation of a PBL activity).

□ Critical friend team asks questions to clarify the desired outcomes and the practice.

□ Critical friend team provides feedback about what seems significant about the practice.

□ Critical friend team provides constructive feedback— raises questions or makes suggestions to guide the learner team to consider higher objectives, to see things from a different perspective, or to make the process more effective. Critical friends try to come up with a solution to any problem they find or work with the learner team to figure out a solution.

◻ Both learner and critical friend teams reflect and write. The critical friend team writes to the learner team with suggestions appropriate to the desired outcomes. The learner team makes notes on the conference.

In general, the learner team needs the critical friend team to provide only constructive feedback, without judging; to listen actively, taking time to understand the "big picture" and the process of planning or implementing; and to advocate for their success and the success of the work of the community of practice.

How can we further refine our task and problem?

Following a check for coherence and feedback from others, you may find it necessary to rethink and refine the task or the problem. In all likelihood, this will mean a small but meaningful rewording of the broad task or problem. It could, however, mean a more substantive reworking of the task or problem. Keep in mind that it is better to make the refinements now rather than once the unit is underway. It is especially helpful to state the problem in the form of an open-ended question to pose to students.

Now that we've defined the task and problem, how do we provide for student codevelopment?

Stating the problem as an open-ended question will better enable you to anticipate possible student generated problems and tasks of interest. From the perspectives of a diverse group of students, what kinds of subproblems and tasks does the question suggest? Of course, brainstorming responses is easiest if you know your students, but it can be a helpful way to anticipate student-generated problems and tasks even if you do not know them. (It may be useful to return to earlier lists of student knowledge, strengths, and interests.) The purpose of this brainstorming is not to set the subproblems, as you have the broad task and problem. Instead, it enables teams to appreciate better the depth and range of possible responses and to begin planning for ways to support students in their identification and investigation of subproblems and tasks.

What other things would be helpful to anticipate before we plan for the actual day-to-day classroom instruction?

Brainstorming possible student-generated problems for later small group inquiry will enable you to anticipate needed roles, assessments, and logistics for this specific PBL unit. In order to support student codevelopment, it will be helpful to consider the ways in which student and teacher roles might change. As described in Goal 2 and in the PBL profiles that follow, teachers become facilitators, guides, and often co-investigators. Students become explorers, evaluators, teachers, and producers. Now is a good time to begin generating roles appropriate to your problems and tasks.

The development of student and teacher roles as well as the roles of others—resource specialists, experts-in-the-field, parents, and community members—will help in identifying useful human, technological, and material resources and learning sites in and out of school. Considering a range of resources and learning sites now will enable you to make any necessary advance arrangements. You and your students will be less likely to encounter roadblocks once the investigations are underway.

It is also important to anticipate how best to measure student progress throughout the unit and determine how well the PBL unit is working. Although it is important to involve students in the development of as many of the specific assessment criteria and tools as possible, it is essential for you to develop the overall evaluation plan—the general assessment criteria and formats. A PBL-CD template of outcomes and assessments, located in Appendix B, is intended for you to use or adapt when planning assessments for the PBL unit and aligning them with overall student outcomes. This template can be used as a draft now. It can then be finalized once instruction is underway.

Given all the considerations in this and earlier steps, a somewhat detailed timeline for the unit of study can now be created.

Although there is a logical sequence to this preliminary planning tool, it is intended to be used flexibly by teams of teachers. We encourage you to give careful consideration to all aspects of planning, but we realize that teams may approach it differently and may revisit one or more aspects of the planning process.

Once you have considered many or all aspects of preliminary planning, it will be helpful to share once again ideas with a critical friend team and to reflect upon and refine your ideas before moving to the next phase of curriculum development. It is this progressive problem solving process of understanding, planning, sharing, reflecting, rethinking, and refining that will build expertise in problem-based teaching and learning.

The pictorial scenario in Figure 4 provides a glimpse of how this preliminary planning process might play out for Bill, Carmen, and their teammates as they prepare for their second PBL unit.

PROBLEM-BASED LEARNING AS CODEVELOPMENT: PLANNING AND IMPLEMENTING THE TEACHING AND LEARNING PROCESS

Whereas the first stage of the PBL-CD model involves preliminary planning that takes place well before instruction, the second major stage of the PBL-CD model is that of planning and implementing the actual day-to-day teaching and learning of the PBL unit. Traditionally, lesson planning was considered complete when nearly everything was accounted for by the teacher—curricular materials, instructional strategies, and specific assessments. Ironically, in PBL, teachers purposefully plan for the unknown—that is, the students' contributions to the problem solving process.

Integration of the Progressive Problem Solving Cycle

The progressive problem solving cycle—the underlying structure of PBL—together with carefully chosen instructional strategies to support that structure enable teachers

PROBLEM-BASED LEARNING AS CODEVELOPMENT: PRELIMINARY PLANNING SCENARIO

Step 1

Figure 4 *Pictorial scenario. Copyright B. Jones, C. Rasmussen, and M. Moffitt, (1995). North Central. Regional Educational Laboratory, Oak Brook, IL. Used by permission.*

Step 2

LATER THAT MORNING . . .

Figure 4 *Continued*

Step 3

Figure 4 *Continued*

Steps 4 & 5

Figure 4 *Continued*

Steps 6 & 7

Figure 4 *Continued*

Figure 4 *Continued*

to achieve their primary goal for students: to engage them in progressive problem solving around an authentic problem and task. Problem solving, as the teacher team has come to experience it in preliminary unit planning, is now integrated into classroom instruction. The fundamental thinking processes of understanding a problem, question, or issue and planning an action, acting on a plan, working toward a preferred outcome, sharing work, reflecting on the work, and rethinking and refining the work, are purposely planned for throughout the five phases of a PBL unit as shown in Figure 5.

Teams of students engage in progressive problem solving in response to a broad task and open-ended question by

◻ identifying specific problems of meaning to them

◻ developing a plan of inquiry or work to investigate a problem of interest

◻ conducting the inquiry and analysis

◻ preparing and presenting findings to one or more authentic audiences

◻ debriefing and consolidating their learning.

So, what will PBL look like on Monday? What instructional strategies will truly support the five phases of the teaching and learning process?

We recognize that PBL-CD will play out differently in every classroom every day of the week. However, let's return to the question and answer format in order to take a closer look at what a team of teachers might consider when planning and implementing the teaching and learning process.

Phase 1. How can we facilitate student understanding of the broad task and problem? How can we encourage students to pursue this study? In what ways can we guide students in identifying specific subproblems?

Progressive Problem – Solving to Build Expertise

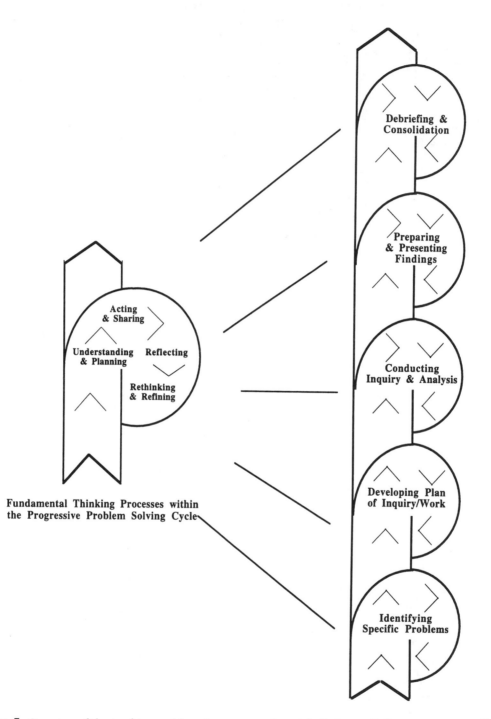

Figure 5 *Overview of the teaching and learning process. Copyright B. Jones, C. Rasmussen, M. Moffitt. (1995). North Central Regional Educational Laboratory, Oak Brook, IL. Used by permission.*

You can. . .

☐ introduce the broad task and pose the open-ended question with any necessary background information. Ideally, you would do so in a way that "hooks" the students, creates the need and desire to learn more about the problem, encourages them to discover or experience the dilemma firsthand, or facilitates their understanding of the problem and its importance

☐ establish what students already know and examine the problem from multiple perspectives

☐ codevelop, with students, specific problems for further inquiry

☐ establish inquiry groups around open-ended subproblems and questions

☐ identify, with students, collaborative skills and monitor their practice of skills

Phase 2. How can we support students in developing a plan of inquiry or work for specific problems?

You can model the planning process and guide students as they . . .

☐ generate predictions, hypotheses, and theories to address their subproblems

☐ identify learning goals

☐ explore potential sources of information and inquiry processes

☐ design a plan of work

☐ identify likely audiences

☐ codevelop, with you, processes to monitor and evaluate their plan

Phase 3. In what ways can we support teams of students as they are conducting their inquiry and analyzing their findings? How can we monitor their progress?

You can . . .

☐ encourage students to reflect on their research, share findings, and gather feedback within and between collaborative groups

☐ encourage students to revise hypotheses or predictions throughout their inquiry

☐ check for progress of inquiry and need for new resources with students

☐ codevelop, with students, plans for specific performance-based assessments

Phase 4. In what ways can we support students when preparing and presenting findings?

By assuming the roles of coach, monitor, and evaluator, you can encourage students to . . .

☐ consolidate theories and findings and revise understandings

☐ revisit and finalize plans for sharing findings

☐ evaluate products and presentations against benchmarks and feedback from others

☐ share findings with authentic audiences

Phase 5. How can we support the debriefing and consolidation of learnings from collaborative groups and the whole group?

While guiding and evaluating, you can work with students to. . .

◻ gather feedback from audiences

◻ identify learnings regarding content, skills, and technology

◻ relate learnings from small groups to each other and to the broad problem and task of the whole group

◻ revisit earlier predictions, hypotheses, and theories and make revisions

◻ consider implications, applications, and any next steps

Let's look in again on our fictional teacher teams. This time we join Bill, Carmen, Coretta, and Eric with their students on the first day of a new PBL unit, and we follow them as they move through their quarter-long investigation. In this scenario, we get a glimpse of each of the five phases of the problem solving process in action.

On the first day of the Winter quarter, the team of Bill, Carmen, Coretta, and Eric share some video clips with each of the two seventh grade classes. The clips show scenes of bounty and productivity, including some shots of the school garden taken this past summer and fall, and scenes of agricultural inefficiency, environmental devastation, and famine. The last clip of the video poses the question, "If our harvest is so bountiful, why is there so much starvation in our world?"

Using a KWHL approach, the class begins by discussing what they *Know* about this problem, sharing prior knowledge and knowledge gained from the video. This information is recorded on easel paper and posted in the room. After exploring all aspects of their present knowledge of the problem, students brainstorm what they *Want* to know more about and what they

Wonder about this problem. These questions for study are also posted along with preliminary ideas for *How* to find out about them.

The room is buzzing throughout these first two days. Students are clearly moved by the video. They are disturbed by much of its content and other evidence of such contrasting situations in their world, locally and globally. Yet, their agitation quickly turns into a commitment to do something about the problem. By the end of day two, various categories of information are organized by students and they are beginning to identify their subquestions of interest.

Bill and Carmen establish inquiry groups, on the basis of the students' interests. Activity alternates between small group planning and refining of plans for their investigation and whole group skill building and debriefing. Bill and Carmen review methods and processes for gathering and analyzing information and graphing data with the whole class. They also have kids practice using critical thinking skills to interpret accurately data. Coretta and Eric organize instructional activities in their classes in ways that would support the investigations, grouping and regrouping students as needed to build skills and help students make connections within and among subject areas. Everyone continues to work on their collaborative social skills and practices interview techniques.

Together, students and teachers create tools for collecting data, recording ideas and interpretations, and evaluating progress. Both teachers and students will use these tools to compare notes during weekly debriefing conferences and the final assessment conference. By the end of the second week, interest-based teams are eager to start their actual investigations.

As the quarter progresses, Bill and Carmen's classroom becomes a growing hub of activity. One of the groups is comparing "old" and "new" methods of agriculture and their feasibility locally and globally. Another group is exploring cultural values and their impact on productivity. Yet another group is investigating the impact of misuse of land on the environment and its long-term implications for people. Still another group is preparing for experimentation with methods of extending productivity beyond the natural growing season.

Bill and Carmen play a variety of roles—monitoring small group work, scheduling student use of the sole school hook-up to the Internet, helping students gain access to on-line resources and e-mail addresses of pertinent organizations and experts, coplanning a field trip to Ball Seed's research facility, and facilitating regular debriefing sessions. Carmen, in particular, relishes her role as colearner in the face-to-face interview of Ball Seed's Educational Foundation Director and in the on-going e-mail dialogue with their scientists. As a former Peace Corp volunteer, Bill enjoys becoming an active co-investigator with students. Together they interview a social ethicist who deals with the environmental and economic concerns of poor people nationally and internationally. Bill's experience in the Peace Corp also makes him a primary resource of information to several groups of students.

Midway through the quarter, each team is studying a different question and is at a different stage of their investigation. Yet, every group is working toward the same goal of a high quality multimedia presentation of their findings and recommendations, as well as making plans for "publishing" these with audiences beyond the school.

As the quarter draws to a close, groups take turns making their culminating presentations, first to their classmates and then to the entire seventh grade, their principal, and invited experts, policymakers, and community members.

The day after the last of these, Bill gathers the group of Cheree, Tiffany, and Juan for their final assessment conference. Each student arrives prepared with a journal and an individual self-assessment. They also bring their collection of graphs, charts, and other artifacts representing their group's quarter-long investigation. As this group had planned, Juan begins by asking each member to reflect on the group's strengths, including their content knowledge, technology use, and social skills. Cheree synthesizes all of the responses, which Tiffany then records on the group self-assessment form. A similar process is followed when reflecting on needed improvement, knowledge gained from other groups' findings and from the audience, and areas for additional investigation. Bill provides observations and insights throughout the conference. He also poses questions to help the students make connections to the broad question of bounty versus starvation and to stimulate ideas for further study.

The collaborative assessment is used for the group portion of each student's grade. Following the conference, Bill reviews each student's journal and self-assessment as well as his log from throughout the quarter. He uses these references to prepare the individual portion of each student's grade. Bill also recalls the "big ideas" students had identified during whole group debriefing when the entire teacher team had revisited the KWHL, asking students to identify what they had *Learned* about the broad problem and task. Student grades, the KWHL, and the ongoing concepts maps enable him to look at the overall success of the class with this problem-based investigative study.

The quarter may end, but the story continues .The instructional team discusses results of the student assessment conferences and their own reflections on the quarter. Then they schedule their appointment with their principal, Beverly, to discuss next steps.

It is impossible to capture all aspects of planning and implementing problem-based learning and teaching in a brief scenario. So, we have also included a five page illustration of the teaching and learning process in Appendix C. The illustration describes in some detail the possible teacher roles and teaching strategies together with corresponding students roles and learning strategies for each PBI phase. A list of "generic" strategies for knowledge building, collaboration, concept representation, reflection, and assessment—all important instructional strategies in PBL—is provided at the end of the chart.

The illustration also incorporates suggested flexible groupings within each phase. When grouping flexibly, teachers group and regroup students according to the purposes of instruction. In a problem-based study, much of the grouping alternates between whole group activities and the ongoing work of small interest groups. Teachers determine when whole group planning would facilitate the work of small interest groups as well as when small groups would benefit from sharing their knowledge with each other in a whole group setting. They also decide when individuals or groups need to come together for skill development. Depending upon the purposes of instruction, students work in a variety of groupings throughout a problem-based study.

In the upcoming chapters you will see a wide variety of groupings, student and teacher roles, and teaching and learning strategies in the context of diverse authentic problem-based learning units. The experiences of these educators and their students are, of course, the best representations of both the richness and the complexity of planning for and implementing problem-based learning.

SELF-DIRECTED ACTIVITIES

1a **Understanding and Planning for Interdisciplinary Teaming:**

☐ Identify the subject areas for a potential interdisciplinary problem-based unit. You may want to use the same unit analyzed in Goal 2 or select or create another unit.

☐ What other teachers might become a part of your planning team?

☐ Look back through the pictorial scenario. What insights, concerns, and questions were brought up by Bill, Carmen, Eric, and Coretta?

☐ What kinds of conversation might take place among the members of your planning team?

1b Understanding and Planning the PBL-CD Unit:

If possible, complete this activity with your planning team members, using whatever form of planning and record-keeping will be most helpful to you. If you or your team are new to interdisciplinary problem-based unit planning, we invite you to use the Preliminary Planning Flowchart in a step-by-step manner. If you or your team have engaged in such unit planning before, we invite you use the Flowchart to consider those aspects of planning that are less familiar to you.

☐ How do we set the parameters for our PBL unit? (subject areas; standards; research base; time and resources)

☐ What other things should we consider before identifying likely problems for study (e.g., content-specific concepts and skills; student needs, strengths, knowledge, interest, and roles; cross-curricular strategies and skills)?

☐ What broad problem and task do we really want students to study?

☐ How coherent are our problems and tasks with our curriculum and instruction?

☐ What kinds of feedback will be helpful and who can provide it?

☐ How can we further refine our task and problem?

☐ How will we provide for student codevelopment?

☐ What other things would be helpful to anticipate before we plan for day-to-day instruction (e.g., roles, resources, assessments, learning sites, timelines)?

2 **Acting and Sharing**: When you have considered many or all of the aspects of preliminary unit planning, share your ideas with a critical friend team. Describe your plans for your informal conference below.

The process for a critical friend dialogue should include:

☐ sharing your desired outcome for the conversation
☐ asking your critical friend to practice active listening and ask clarifying questions
☐ asking your critical friend to offer constructive, nonjudgmental feedback

3 **Reflecting**: Reflect upon the outcomes of your critical friend conference. List or in some way represent them (metaphor, graphic organizer, icon).

4 **Rethinking and Refining**: What are the implications for you or your team's unit plan?

Next Steps . . . You or your team may now be ready to take the next steps of planning for the day to day activities of the classroom. Goals Four through Seven offer examples of PBL-CD units. The Self-Directed Activities that follow each of these goals invite you or your team to engage in two types of study: exploring the content of these units for useful applications and practicing the progressive problem-solving process in relation to the further planning of your curriculum unit.

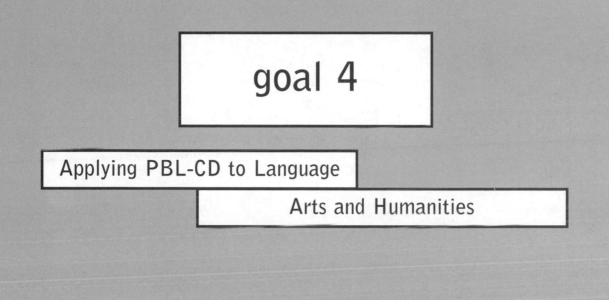

goal 4

Applying PBL-CD to Language
Arts and Humanities

This Goal illustrates very different approaches to problem-based learning in the humanities in middle schools. Whereas Rasmussen's Profile for language arts, "How Are Perceptions of the Homeless Changing?", is essentially a reflection on a unit previously taught, the Profile entitled "How Do We Make a Proposal for a Public Sculpture?" uses the PBL-CD framework to design a unit that has not been taught.

The language arts Profile, designed for a traditional junior high school, represents a relatively small first step toward problem-based learning that makes a big difference in student outcomes. Rasmussen, then a teacher, had developed a mini unit focusing on the homeless. To address the open-ended question of how perceptions of the homeless are changing, eighth-grade students explored current and past perceptions as well as their own personal perceptions. The research component involved combining PBL with applications of whole language approaches and cooperative learning. Thinking skills and study skills were threaded throughout the unit. This is a good example of problem-based learning that takes place fully in school, does not require technology, and makes the most of a self-contained literature class.

The Profile on making a proposal for a public sculpture envisions students working through the various processes that a professional sculptor would go through to submit a proposal for a community sculpture. The author, himself an artist, uses the PBL-CD framework to design a unit that had not yet been taught at the time of writing this book. The design of the unit was informed by research on using art to develop multiple intelligences. Students will work directly with the artist as apprentices and will go out of school to present their sculpture design to an audience of community leaders. This Profile design incorporates mathematics, history, science, language arts, and communication skills, using various technologies as tools throughout the study.

HOW ARE PERCEPTIONS OF THE HOMELESS CHANGING? MAKING WHOLE LANGUAGE MORE PROBLEM BASED

Claudette Rasmussen, *Marie Murphy School*

Overview of the Project
The overall goal of this two week mini-unit was to make the content of a literature class in a traditionally structured junior high school more meaningful and integrative for students. I felt that making the whole language approach that

I had always used more problem-based would be a natural means of accomplishing that goal. A very rich short story about the experience of homelessness that had been a part of my curriculum for some time became the inspiration for our problem-based study. Following an interpretive discussion of this story, I posed this question to students for investigation: "How are perceptions of the homeless changing?"

Students explored their own and others' perceptions of the homeless using a variety of print resources, including factual articles about the conditions of homelessness and firsthand accounts of homelessness in Chicago and the United States. Their own changing perceptions of the homeless became the stimulus for the first creative work in their writing portfolios for the class.

All students were very engaged in the literature discussion and the subsequent study of related writings. They shared personal observations and experiences, posed many thoughtful questions, and expressed numerous concerns about the conditions of homelessness. Many wrote moving creative stories as a result of their investigations.

This relatively small change in my whole language curriculum had a big impact on the involvement of the students, enhancing their understanding of a socially significant problem and enriching their use of reading, writing, speaking, and listening skills. In addition to the creative role of producer, students became each others' teachers in their collaborative investigation. My role was that of facilitator and, at times, colearner as we all strived to understand better the personal and societal implications of this problem.

Although this unit took place in one eighth grade classroom in 1991, its goal and many of its instructional approaches became representative of how I taught reading and literature classes in grades four through eight within an enrichment program. Most, if not all, of these interdisciplinary, problem-based, whole language approaches would be beneficial for all students, regardless of age or ability.

I felt that the applications of many of these approaches across ages, abilities, and subject areas as well as the high impact that resulted from relatively small changes in curriculum and instruction were worth sharing in this book. Making whole language more problem-based had a profound effect on my students and on me, and I think it has many implications for other teachers' use of interdisciplinary, problem-based practices.

DESCRIPTION OF THE SCHOOL

Marie Murphy School is a junior high school in a school district of approximately 600 students, K–8, in an affluent suburb north of the city of Chicago. At the time of this unit, its student population was approximately 25% Asian and 75% Caucasian, including immigrants from Japan, Korea, eastern Europe, and Mediterranean countries.

At that time, I was the Coordinator of and a Teacher in the Pupil Enrichment Program. I worked with classroom teachers throughout the district to integrate enrichment activities into the regular classroom and taught enrichment classes for students of high ability in grades 4 through 8. I had been integrating thinking skills with content skills and combining individual as well as small and whole group instruction for many of the fourteen years I had been in education. What was new to this unit was its focus on a significant problem with broad implications.

RATIONALE FOR THE PROJECT

Purpose

When considering the overall goal of this unit—that is, to make literature more integrated and meaningful for students—making whole language more problem-based seemed to me to be a natural means of accomplishing that goal. Using literature as a catalyst for examining problems of interest to students, while applying reading, writing, speaking, and listening skills provided integration and meaning. Choosing a real-life problem of social significance, like that of homelessness, and incorporating many creative and critical thinking skills added still more integration, authenticity, and challenge.

Research

Despite the fact that I was teaching in a traditionally organized junior high school, I was committed to teaching my literature course following beliefs and principles of whole language (Goodman, 1986). I support the fundamental belief that the function of language is to construct meaning (Altwerger, Edelsky, & Flores, 1987). I have always been a believer in a holistic language approach. My commitment came first from a common sense examination of how accomplished learners develop their literacy skills naturally. For example, it seems most natural to build vocabulary when encountering new words while reading. It also seems natural that it is the reader, not the teacher or the publisher, that can best identify the words that are new to him or her, the words it is necessary to know in order to comprehend a story. Similarly, it is natural for a writer to refine grammar and spelling skills while editing his or her own writing, motivated by the need to share original work. This approach is consistent with a whole language philosophy devoted to nurturing students' literacy development where literature and a student's own writing provide the context for skill development. ". . . Children are taught about the parts of language while they pursue 'authentic' reading and writing." (Willis, 1995, p. 1) Teaching skills in the context of high-quality, whole works of literature represents a basic tenet of whole language.

Reading for meaning, writing often, and writing well are also tenets of this approach. Again it seemed most natural as well as consistent with the whole language philosophy to develop an understanding and appreciation of the author's intent in a story by interpreting his or her writing and by engaging in writing as an outgrowth of that interpretative reading and discussion. So, although my students were enrolled in a separate language arts class with another teacher for which they had writing assignments, they were expected to write in response to what they were reading in my literature class. Given their "double dose" of writing, a problem-focused study seemed especially meaningful and motivating.

The question "How are perceptions of the homeless changing?" has many of the hallmarks of both problem-based and project-based learning. It engages students in the investigation, however informal, of a real-world problem by gathering information, communicating ideas and findings, refining perceptions, and creating artifacts. So, this literature classroom became the site of an informal investigation of perceptions of the homeless.

One of the primary strategies used for small group investigation in this mini-unit was the jigsawing of print materials on homelessness (described in the section entitled "Flow of the Project"). This jigsaw method was just one of the many cooperative learning strategies that I used regularly in my classroom. I had completed both basic and leadership training with Johnson, Johnson, and Holubec (1988) in their conceptual approach to cooperative learning. This approach, based on theories of cooperation and competition, provided general principles that enabled teachers to analyze their curriculum and instruction and structure cooperative learning activities to meet a wide range of needs. It emphasized cooperative learning groups based on positive interdependence among group members; individual accountability; typically heterogeneous membership; completing a task while maintaining good working relationships (product and process); shared leadership; shared responsibility for each other's success; the direct teaching of social skills; the teacher observing and monitoring group work, intervening only when necessary; and the groups debriefing their effectiveness. The jigsaw technique (Aronson, 1978) was one way of structuring positive interdependence among group members by collaboratively learning and teaching a variety of materials.

Within the context of a whole language experience, eighth grade students began collaboratively investigating the pressing social problem of homelessness. Their responses to the problem-based study reinforced my belief that teenagers are genuinely interested in problems of social significance. James Beane, National Louis University, says that those who believe adolescents' interests are trivial and self-centered are often mistaken. Students have "tremendous concerns about the larger world . . . they are very concerned about the future." (quoted in Willis, 1992, p. 4)

Broad Student Outcomes

The approach used to read, analyze, and interpret literature and to write in response to that literature was a part of this and other whole language experiences throughout the course. These language arts instructional strategies addressed several of the Illinois State Goals for grade 8 (Illinois State Board of Education, 1993). These Goals state that as a result of their schooling, students will be able to

☐ understand how language functions and evolves;

☐ read, comprehend, interpret, evaluate, and use a variety of written materials;

☐ listen critically and analytically;

☐ write standard English in a grammatical, well-organized and coherent manner for a variety of purposes.

In this unit many reading, writing, speaking, and listening skills identified as objectives of the Prentice Hall Literature (Prentice Hall, 1989) series used in the regular instructional program were also practiced. Those skills include

☐ reading and appreciating short stories;

☐ becoming familiar with the elements of the short story;

☐ using critical thinking and reading strategies to gain a fuller understanding of short stories;

☐ developing strategies for understanding and appreciating words in a story;

☐ using short stories as a springboard for writing imaginatively and critically.

Many thinking skills and study skills were also refined. A variety of critical thinking skills were required when preparing for and discussing the story—predicting, verifying predictions, interpreting, justifying interpretations, and posing interpretive questions. Reading for meaning and vocabulary study were a natural part of story preparation. Highlighting important text passages, making notes in the margins, and using the dictionary as a tool were a routine part of the preparation.

Both creative and critical thinking skills were used throughout the stages of the writing process—during prewriting, writing, revising, editing, and "publishing." Students read short stories and primary sources of print material representing a range of writing styles. They were then encouraged to experiment with aspects of these styles in their own writing. More importantly, they were encouraged to give creative voice to their imagination and personal beliefs.

Many collaborative skills were practiced throughout whole group discussion, peer review of student writing, and small group investigations. In many ways students were teaching and learning together by continually exploring different perspectives and evaluating their significance.

Most importantly, knowledge and skills were applied to the study of a real-life problem of social significance and of genuine interest to students. Investigating changing perceptions of the homeless enabled us to build effectively on students' prior knowledge, stimulate many thinking processes, and explore the social, political, and economic ramifications of this problem. Reflections on the problem of homelessness throughout the unit contributed to a personal, and often poignant, expression of understanding.

Ill-Structured Problem or Question and Broad Task

The short story, "Waiting for Her Train," had been a part of my curriculum for some time. It is a story rich in symbolism and multiple meanings about the perceptions of a homeless woman. I had always considered its unexpected revelations and symbolism to be very powerful. And the story, though written some time ago, seemed more current than ever in its subject matter. The way in which this story dealt with the experience of homelessness seemed rich for further study. I chose the question "How are perceptions

of the homeless changing?" for students to investigate because of the continuing impact of homelessness on society,
and because I felt this social issue would be of concern to
them. By wording the problem as an open-ended question
about perceptions, students were able to gather information about all aspects of the problem and explore past and
present perceptions of the homeless. That investigative
task, within the context of the fictional short story and
other non fictional firsthand accounts of homelessness,
prompted students to reflect and write about their own
changing perceptions of the homeless.

Assessment

Students were asked to write creatively about their perceptions of the homeless. Their final draft, and all the artifacts of their writing process, were among the works
collected in a portfolio. At the trimester's end, students
selected their best works for self- and teacher-assessment.
Portfolio work represented nearly half of each student's
grade. Individual preparation for and participation in discussion, small group work, and vocabulary use made up
the remainder of the grade.

FLOW OF THE PROJECT

I began the trimester with a Directed Reading Thinking Activity (DRTA) designed to engage students in active listening and thinking about a short story. At carefully selected
points in the oral reading of the story, "Waiting for Her
Train," I asked students to "stop and think"—to make predictions about possible outcomes and then, following the
next segment, to justify and refine their predictions on the
basis of evidence from the story or from real life. Rather
than handling this story as an isolated literature activity, I
selected a literary work that reflected a pressing social problem that all of my students had encountered in some way.

For homework, the students were expected to do a
careful second reading of the story, highlighting significant
passages and reacting or making interpretive comments in
the margins. Vocabulary study was a natural outgrowth of

words encountered while reading, and students were expected to generate their own list of new words and appropriate definitions.

As always, the short story was followed by two days of interpretive discussion where students would respond to open-ended Socratic questions about the story's meaning and support their answers with evidence from the text and from real life. The Socratic questions were both teacher- and student-generated.

Following DRTA, independent reading, and interpretive discussion, students were asked to write informally about their present experiences with and perceptions of the homeless.

Then students were divided into cooperative learning groups to investigate further perceptions of the homeless using a variety of print resources. Resources included factual articles written about the condition of homelessness in Chicago and the United States; articles written by Chicago journalists who had gone "underground" to observe the homeless and experience homelessness; and firsthand accounts of homelessness, in poetry and prose form, published by the Chicago Coalition for the Homeless. A jigsaw technique was used, whereby students were assigned to a "home" group. After numbering-off from one to four within that group, each student joined others of like number in an "expert" group (e.g., the ones from each of the home groups became an expert group). Each expert group was then assigned some of the print material to study. They were expected to determine how to work together to read the material, summarize important information using an outline or graphic organizer, and create a visual representing one or more of the most important ideas. Students then returned to their home group to share their expertise with one another. In this way, students covered a lot of information in a relatively short period of time by teaching and learning with each other.

Following whole group debriefing about significant learnings and their implications, students were again asked to write informally about their changing perceptions of the homeless.

Their perceptions became the stimulus for the first creative work in their writing portfolios. The first draft of their writing went through peer review—where one or more students reacted to the writing by citing strengths, posing questions, and making recommendations—and one or more revisions.

STUDENT EXAMPLE AND SAMPLE ACTIVITY

The students' responsiveness to this mini-unit was typified by Noam. Noam was especially active in this literature discussion, sharing his interpretations of the story and his observations of the homeless. Prior to cooperative group work, Noam brought in a copy of "Streetwise," a newspaper written by some of Chicago's homeless and sold on street corners throughout the metropolitan area. He eagerly shared excerpts from the publication with his classmates. He was very involved in the investigation of other print resources. Noam later wrote a very moving first-person fictional account of one man's encounter with homelessness. He refined his writing through several drafts and selected it as one of the "best works" in his portfolio at the trimester's end.

The use of portfolios, within the context of a whole language classroom, provided valuable insights into the writing process and into the students-as-authors for both me and my students. The use of portfolio writing focused on a real-life problem was especially powerful in giving creative voice to students' beliefs. An example of my instructions to students for the organization and evaluation of their writing portfolios is given in Exhibit 2.

REFLECTION AND SELF-ASSESSMENT

For a short unit, making whole language more problem-based went a long way toward accomplishing my initial goal of more meaningful and integrative instruction and toward achieving a vision of engaged learning as described in this book.

The students were clearly responsible for their own learning in individual preparation, small group investiga-

EXHIBIT 2 | Portfolio Power

To turn your binder into a portfolio,

1. Arrange all your works of writing from most to least effective, including all evidence of the writing process behind each final draft.

2. Reflect on your two best works, and on a separate sheet of paper for each work, answer the following questions:

☐ What makes this your best (second best) work?

☐ How did you go about writing it?

☐ What problems did you encounter?

☐ How did you solve them?

☐ What goals did you set for yourself?

☐ How did you go about accomplishing them?
Place this evaluation of your process and product in front of each final draft when completed.

3. Answer these two questions on a single sheet of paper at the front of your portfolio.

☐ What makes your most effective work different from your least effective work?

☐ What are your goals for future writing?

4. Include an illustrated cover or title page and a table of contents at the beginning of your portfolio.
   Your self-evaluation of your two best works will be as important to your grade as my assessment of your final two drafts and their writing process. I will also consider the number of works in your portfolio, the range of styles, and your progress as a writer.

tion, and whole group discussion. Students were collaborative, working with different partners for each "peer review" of an original story and working in a variety of small groups throughout the trimester. Grouping was structured by me to encourage multiple perspectives and to be as heterogeneous as possible. It was also flexible in response to the varying purposes of instruction. The students, as represented by Noam, were energized by learning. I think that was due primarily to the challenging, authentic task, which was socially significant and of interest to students. Assessment was seamless and ongoing, performance-based, and equitable. Multiple measures were used; both process and product were evaluated; students were aware of the standards as they applied to all; and they were involved in self-assessment. Implicit in the students' portfolio self-assessment was the development of criteria for effective writing. In that way, student assessment was generative. Nearly all of the instructional strategies were also generative and interactive, including (a) the use of Socratic dialogue during interpretive discussion, (b) the jigsaw technique for small group investigation with its emphasis on graphic representations and reciprocal teaching, (c) whole group debriefing that followed the investigation, (d) and writing for reflection on personal perceptions of the homeless and as a creative outlet for beliefs and newly acquired knowledge.

Although the classroom itself functioned as a knowledge-building learning community, this unit would have been strengthened by reaching beyond the classroom walls to the authors and professionals directly involved in issues of homelessness. Even though the political, economic, physical and mental health, and other societal implications of homelessness were discussed during debriefing activities, student-generated questions would have resulted in more in-depth study. For example, one small group may have decided to focus their study on changing perceptions of and by homeless children. Another group may have wanted to examine the causes of and responses to increasing numbers of homeless women and children. The sharing of results of several related investigations would have made even greater contributions to the collective knowledge and, in all likelihood, stimulated a wider range of creative writing. The multidisciplinary nature of the task would also have been strengthened through active connections with other subject areas within school. Involvement in a community service project would have been a powerful culminating learning experience and made the unit an even more authentic task.

The strengths of this problem-based whole language unit, together with the suggested improvements, would enable both student and teacher roles to be expanded. In addition to their roles as teachers and producers of knowledge, students would be able to become more active explorers and possibly even cognitive apprentices in investigations that extend beyond the classroom. In addition to the teacher roles of facilitator and guide, I would be able to be more of a co-investigator along with the students.

HOW DO WE MAKE A PROPOSAL FOR A PUBLIC SCULPTURE?

Ted Injasulian, *Robert Abbott Middle School for the Fine and Applied Arts and Sciences*

Overview of the Project

In this unit, eighth grade students will develop a proposal for an original sculpture for a specific environment within the city of Waukegan. A local area artist will collaborate with students on this project, acting as role model, mentor, and consultant. Subject areas that will be integrated into this art-based project include (a) mathematics for measurements and cost projections, (b) history for the study of past and present sculptures constructed in the area, (c) science for geology of the proposed site and the effects of weather, and (d) language arts for the writing and communication skills needed for proposal development and presentation. Technology will be used as a tool throughout this study in the form of camcorders, computer cameras, scanners, specialized software for designing the artwork, and digitized animation for presentation purposes. Upon completion of the proposal, the students, artist, principal, and art teacher will make their recommendation to city council members for its acceptance or rejection.

Through this problem-based study, students will learn the process of creating an artwork—the same process an artist goes through to get a public sculpture made. This process will involve taking an idea and developing its structure, visualizing it in an environment, doing research on all the variables needed to construct the idea, and presenting it to an authentic audience for possible funding of materials and permissions for construction. Most importantly, students will work collaboratively within a small group and as a whole class alongside a practicing artist, teachers, and community leaders to bring their proposed sculpture closer to reality.

By experiencing this, it is hoped that students will gain a better appreciation of this artform and an understanding of why sculpture is important in the everyday life of people. It is anticipated that students will also heighten their expectations, become more aware of their talents, recognize that they have the ability to improve the environment in which they live, and gain insight into some ways in which collaborative relationships can support their goals.

DESCRIPTION OF THE SCHOOL

Robert Abbott Middle School for the Fine and Applied Arts and Sciences is an urban school for grades 6 through 8 located in the downtown section of Waukegan, Illinois. The school first opened in 1992 and, like all elementary schools in Waukegan, draws students from the neighborhood and throughout the city who are interested in its theme. The student population is made up primarily of low socio-economic students. Of our students, 75% are on free and reduced lunch; 69% of our families are considered low income. Within the school, the percentages of students according to ethnic group are 70% Hispanic, 20% African American, 7% Caucasian, and 3% Asian. Of the school's population, 26% is limited English proficient. Approximately 55% of our students would qualify for Chapter 1 services (government-supported remedial intruction in reading and mathematics). This information reflects the range of special needs of our students and their cultural diversity. Although our students often come to Abbott with an interest in the arts, they seldom have prior experience in the arts and sciences and enter as novices.

I am the art teacher and resident artist for Abbott Middle School. I have always approached art instruction from a multidisciplinary perspective. Recently, the thematic, interdisciplinary curriculum development that has been a part of my instructional program and of many of my colleagues' programs across the district has become more problem-focused. This unit reflects that emphasis on problem-based teaching and learning. Jo Williamson, the district middle schools Technology Coordinator, and Claudette Rasmussen, one of the authors of this book, collaborated in the writing of this profile.

RATIONALE FOR THE UNIT

Purpose

This project is designed to exemplify the importance of sculpture in the everyday life of people. It is also intended as an avenue for students to build an appreciation of this artform and the creative problem-solving process of making a proposal for an original sculpture for the city. Whether the proposal is accepted or rejected, it is meant to engage students in an authentic task in much the same way a practicing artist might experience it and to raise their expectations of what they can do, as individuals and as a group, in collaboration with professionals and with each other.

Research

Howard Gardner's book, *Art Education and Human Development* (1990), was used as the basis for this project. The Indiana school, Key Elementary, was also a point of inspiration for its curricular application of Gardner's multiple intelligences theory. His emphasis on multiple intelligences and the significance of art to human development and activity has reinforced my belief that visual art forms, integrated with other discipline areas, encourage students to attain success.

Teaching in this manner, with art first in the curriculum, many students comprehend and solve problems easily through hands-on activity, including those students who have traditionally been unsuccessful in core academic subjects. They move more readily from spatial, kinesthetic, and intrapersonal experiences to linguistic, logical, and interpersonal experiences. Moving this way, students engage in a holistic way of learning. This unit is set up to use art to reinforce skills from other domains and to provide practical activities in which to apply principles from other areas of study.

This unit also uses the research on expertise and the recognition that the work of experts-in-the-field is inherently interdisciplinary. The unit is founded on the understanding that expertise involves much more than simply an accumulation of facts about a certain topic, although a great deal of specialized content knowledge is likely to be present in the expert. What may be more important in distinguishing between the novice, the intermediate, and the expert is the way in which content knowledge is organized, reconstructed, and creatively applied. One 7-year study that analyzed the characteristics of expert artists concluded that

> the critical ability which distinguished the successful artists was not terminology, art history, or even technical skill but rather the ability to envision, pose, formulate, or create a new problematic situation. . . . The successful artists explored more of the materials before them and explored them in more depth, fingering, moving, touching, rearranging, and playing with alternatives, versus moving quickly to a rather conventional arrangement and sketch. (Flower & Hayes, 1994, p.73)

The artistic tradition has valued active learning, expertise-building, and strong mentor-student relationships. Some of the more recent social models of mentoring mimic the way arts and crafts masters have trained their students for centuries. Collins, Brown, and Holum's (1991) cognitive apprenticeship approach emphasizes making the thinking processes just as visible as the observable processes involved in the task. Other principles important to this model include creating a learning environment where students are immersed in an authentic task and encouraging students to focus on understanding the whole before executing the parts of the task. Mentors model tasks, coach students, and encourage learners to define and solve their own problems in a collaborative environment.

In this project, the use of a local area sculptor as mentor and collaborator and a wide variety of technology tools to explore and design sculpture, as well as the integration of mathematics, science, history, and language arts into the proposal process all reflect the rich research base described above. More importantly, these factors work together in support of student success with a challenging, authentic task.

Broad Student Outcomes

Students will experience the process of designing and proposing a public sculpture by (a) taking a creative idea and developing its structure, (b) visualizing it in an environment, (c) doing research on all the variables needed to construct the artwork, and (d) presenting it to a public audience for possible funding of materials and permissions for construction. In doing so, students will gain a better understanding of the elements and principles of artistic composition and greater appreciation of this artform. They will also improve their problem-solving capabilities. Students' collaborative skills will be strengthened as they work within small groups to design a sculpture and as a whole class on the proposal for the sculpture of choice. Working alongside the practicing artist will enable students to understand and appreciate the process an artist goes through to get a public sculpture made, especially the importance of the artist's vision in that process, and why sculpture is important in the everyday life of people. It is anticipated that students will grow in their awareness of their own talents and the talents of their classmates and their own ability to improve the environment in which they live.

Students will use other disciplines to investigate variables in this art-based project: mathematics for measurements, cost projections, and allocations to contractors; history for the study of past and present sculptures constructed in the area; science for geology of the proposed site, effects of weather, and material composition; and language arts for the writing and communication skills needed for proposal development and presentation. Students will develop skill in using a wide range of technological tools in the design and presentation of the proposal for a public sculpture.

Broad Task and Ill-Structured Question

The broad task is incorporated in the broad question itself: How do we make a proposal for a public sculpture?

Assessment

There will be two primary means of assessing student performance in this design and proposal process: an ongoing student journal and artifacts of both the proposal process and its final presentation. Both forms of assessment encourage the integration of skills into bigger concepts and more comprehensive thinking processes.

Six broad criteria will be assessed, including evidence of the application of (a) art elements and principles; (b) reactivity and the work ethic as a part of the artist-apprenticeship relationship; (c) specific software and technology tools; (d) pertinent mathematics, science, history, and language arts skills; (e) ongoing journal entries and complete visual work; and (f) presentation skills.

FLOW OF THE PROJECT, TIMELINE, AND SAMPLE ACTIVITY

Students will move from general to specific—from an understanding of the whole before executing the parts—when approaching this project and learning how to make a proposal for a public sculpture.

1. A teacher-created video will be shown in order to demonstrate the whole design and proposal process and motivate the students. During the "pilot" of this unit, the video will consist of an interview with an actual artist de-

scribing the design and proposal process as well as examples of several public sculptures in the area. In years following, the video will show work done by students engaged in the design and proposal process during the sculpture unit and will include the following images to illustrate the progression:

□ introduction to project

□ students in discussion groups

□ students in environment filming

□ students working with technological tools

□ graphic depicting software and student and artist

□ students working as apprentices to the artist on interdisciplinary skills

□ graphic of sculpture in the environment

□ students critiquing a proposed video

□ students presenting final proposal

2. Students will gain the necessary background knowledge by engaging in a process of discussion, research, and exploration of

□ the elements and principles involved in sculpture, with an emphasis on basic shapes.

□ the technological tools and mediums to be used as replacements for construction materials. Pencils and paper are replaced by computers and specific software. Photographic film and animation by hand in video form are replaced by digitized software. Mediums like wood, metal, paper, clay are replaced by film. Using the more abstract or formal technology tools also facilitates higher order thinking and problem solving skills.

□ the value of the project to students and the community, including the importance of art in their daily lives. The opportunities for leadership, collaboration, and heightened self-awareness will also be discussed.

□ pertinent art history, especially the past and present roles of artists and apprentices.

□ what works and what does not work in their use of technology in preliminary designs. For example, one computer program enables students to experiment with "skins" of different colors and textures for their potential artform; another software allows students to rotate, flip, suspend, compact, and further manipulate their artform as well as cast it in different lights and place it in different contexts. Students will compare and contrast their explorations.

□ real-life dilemmas in which interdisciplinary skills are essential. Students will benefit from the guidance of the mentor artist, when needed.

3. Each small group of students will be given an environment, a tool, and software to design their proposed sculpture and prepare their video. They must decide how to make use of their strengths in this process. The teacher now becomes a coach. Students in this phase may also look to the artist, subject area specialists, and community professionals for assistance.

4. Each group will show their video while other students offer constructive criticism. Problems and potential solutions will be discussed, and refinements will be made.

5. Students will present their proposals, including their revised videos, to their classmates. They will receive immediate feedback from their peers, and the class will select one group's work to represent their best thinking. That proposal will then be presented to the city council for their acceptance or rejection and their feedback. The students, teacher, and artist will debrief what they have learned about

making a proposal for a public sculpture and what they have learned about this artform and its importance in everyday life.

"How do we make a proposal for a public sculpture?" is definitely a semester-long unit. It is estimated that it will take 10 to 20 days for students to complete any one of the following tasks: becoming familiar with the software; conducting the research; developing the sculpture in an environment on the computer in three dimensions; compiling the information in a rough draft, including speech, music, and film; finalizing the project; and presenting it to the city council.

REFLECTION AND SELF-ASSESSMENT

This unit has not yet been taught, so it may therefore be premature to evaluate it. However, when reflecting upon this unit and assessing its effectiveness, it may be helpful to consider the following questions. How appropriate was the level of difficulty? What are some additional ways in which students can have more of a codevelopment role, especially with regard to subquestions and assessment criteria? How might the journal be structured for optimal recording, reflection, and self-assessment?

It is anticipated that this unit will be highly successful because it is interdisciplinary, problem-based, authentic in its task and its audience, and because teachers and students take on meaningful and appropriate roles. Perhaps the biggest questions will be: How can students connect this meaningful learning with subsequent experiences in art, other subject areas, and in their homes and community? How can they sustain their heightened expectations and efficacy?

The second stage of the PBL-CD model, Planning and Implementing the Teaching and Learning Process, involves planning for and implementing five phases of progressive problem solving. These phases are described in detail on pages 73–76 of Goal 3 and in Appendix C. We will move through the five phases of progressive problem solving during the next four sets of self-directed activities. In this activity, we focus on *Phase 1: Identifying Specific Problems*.

1a **Understanding the Teacher Authors' PBL-CD Units:** Compare and contrast ideas from the two PBL-CD units. What useful ideas have these teacher authors incorporated into their PBL-CD units? Which ideas are unique to each unit and which are common to both units? Record them in the appropriate areas of this Venn diagram:

How Are Perceptions of the Homeless Changing?
Making Whole Language More Problem-Based

How Do We Make a Proposal
for a Public Sculpture?

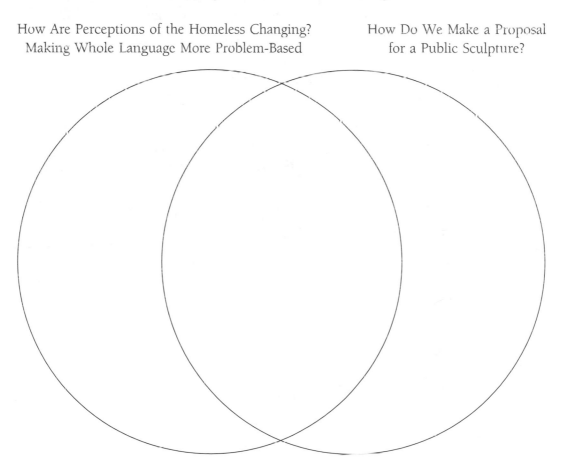

1b **Understanding and Planning for Your PBL-CD Units:** *Phase 1—Identifying Specific Problems.* Using Goal 3 and Appendix C as references, what ideas from the Venn would be most useful to you as you build upon preliminary plans in preparation for Phase 1?

Think about how these ideas as well as your own will help you to prepare for Phase 1 of progressive problem solving in the classroom: What teaching and learning strategies will help you and your students identify specific problems? What teacher roles and student roles will be most appropriate throughout this phase?

Teacher Roles	Teaching Goals and Strategies	Student Roles	Learning Strategies and Responsibilities

2 **Acting and Sharing:** When you have completed a draft of possible instructional activities for Phase 1, share your ideas with a critical friend team. Describe your plans for your informal conference below.
Process for a "critical friend" dialogue:

☐ share your desired outcome for the conversation
☐ ask your critical friend to practice active listening and ask clarifying questions
☐ offer constructive, nonjudgmental feedback

3 **Reflecting:** Reflect upon the outcomes of your critical friend conference. List or in some way represent them (metaphor, graphic organizer, icon).

4 **Rethinking and Refining:** What are the implications for you or your team's unit plan?

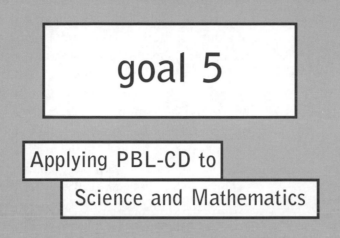

goal 5

Applying PBL-CD to Science and Mathematics

In this Goal, the Profiles focus on problem-based learning in science and mathematics contexts. The two schools profiled are very different in terms of their problems, resources, research, and student populations, yet both utilize rich community resources.

Gladstone Elementary School in Chicago is an inner city school that is home to large numbers of special education students. Additionally, there is an unusually high incidence of asthma and other health problems in the school community. To address issues of health and disability, the school collaborated with a local university to provide a large family and community health center. This unit focuses on how to use problem-based learning to address the asthma problem there. This Family Nursing Center would serve as a major resource throughout the project. Many of the goals and procedures of PESL (project-enhance science learning; Feldman & McWilliams, 1995) fit well with the research component of this unit. To recall from Goal 1 in this book, we described the events that took place in Pease Middle School when they used an air pump to sample the quality of the air at their school and found too much CO_2 in the air. The idea at Gladstone was to use the air pump and the PESL approach to search for the causes of asthma in local air conditions in and around the school. Accordingly, this is a rich interdisciplinary unit with science objectives focusing on technology use and the inquiry process, mathematics objectives focusing on data collection and analysis, as well as language arts and health objectives.

The Museum Project, developed by an elementary school for gifted students in Chicago, emerged in part from access to a major zoo, and in part from discussions focusing on the use if the metaphor of school-as-museum and museum-as-school to describe the nature of informal, highly engaged learning. The initial plan was for Edison to launch into PBL-CD through a large, multigrade project focusing on parallel evolution in biology. The students were to build a small display for a museum that would contain information about toucans and hornbills. Extensive plans were made to develop activities that would enhance students' understanding of the broader concepts related to parallel evolution. The activities would incorporate history as well as science objectives and develop multiple intelligences and abilities. The school was very concerned about making sure that their students were challenged and focused on concepts consistent with high expectations for gifted children. As students, teachers, and others interacted, the focus shifted to the rain forest, the scope of the display escalated, and the project prompted great enthusiasm across the school. Teachers learned a great deal about the process of PBL and have great plans for reteaching this unit.

WHAT CAN WE DO ABOUT ASTHMA IN OUR COMMUNITY?

Delamie Thompson, Paul Gilvary, and Mary Moffitt, *Gladstone Elementary School*

Overview of the Project

The purpose of our project is to involve inner city elementary students in an authentic learning project whereby they investigate causes, incidence, and treatment of a major health problem in the local community: asthma and its related conditions. Through small group inquiry related to an open-ended question, "Why is there so much asthma in our community and what can we do about it?", sixth grade students will gain an understanding of how the environment affects their health. They will then share this understanding and their recommendations with others. The project will take place over one trimester and will involve many subject areas including health, science, math, and the humanities.

Gladstone students will build a common knowledge base related to causes, incidence, and treatment of asthma toward the goal of sharing their findings and recommendations with others who might also benefit. Students will compare the incidence rate of asthma and students' management methods with data gathered from health-related sources and from students at other schools. This will be a powerful learning experience as students formulate and modify guiding questions and conduct their own investigations, analyze research conducted by others, and generate solutions to a real problem.

We have used the indicators of engaged learning and many of the interdisciplinary, problem-based practices described in this book to design this unit.

DESCRIPTION OF THE SCHOOL

Gladstone school is located on Chicago's near west side, an industrial part of the city. Approximately 81% of the 530 students are African American and 18% of the students are Hispanic. Greater than 90% of the student population are from poverty-level homes. This affects students in many ways, including their health. Realizing that students' primary needs must be met before learning can occur, the school has made considerable efforts to become an integral part of the community. Gladstone participates in many innovative community projects including establishment of the Family Nursing Center, which is located in the school building in conjunction with Saint Xavier University School of Nursing. The Nursing Center is funded by a grant from the federal government.

This project was initiated by Paul Gilvary, a science teacher at Gladstone, and Delamie Thompson, Community Nurse Specialist of the Family Nursing Center at Gladstone. Project-based learning is a relatively new idea for teachers at Gladstone, though hands-on and authentic tasks in health units have been part of the school's philosophy in establishing an on-site health center. Therefore one of the authors, Mary Moffitt, collaborated with Paul and Delamie to develop and write this unit.

RATIONALE FOR THE PROJECT

Purpose

The current rate of asthma at Gladstone is 8%, though the actual rate is likely to be higher because inconsistent medical care often leaves asthma underdiagnosed. Studies have shown a higher incidence of asthma in low income areas. It is estimated that nearly 10% of hospital admissions in an inner-city are for asthma related conditions. Scientists speculate that this is due to increased levels of allergens in the air.

Lack of routine medical care and inaccessibility to health-care resources often make for poor management of asthma in the inner-city. Children may present with an asthma episode but have no inhaler, the most effective way to treat an episode. Currently, Gladstone students and families have fairly limited information about asthma and the potential precipitators of an episode, making prevention more difficult. We want our students to understand their condition and to feel safe not only in self-managing, but also in being able to depend on knowledgeable peers and adults when they have an asthma episode at school. This means the entire school community must become familiar with the triggers of and the treatments for asthma.

By identifying and investigating questions related to asthma, children will learn more about how their bodies respond to the environment and to other factors, such as emotions. This chronic health condition can become empowering to a child as he or she gains understanding and learns more about asthma and ways to control it.

Many questions come to mind related to causes, incidence, and treatment of asthma for Gladstone students. Why is our rate of incidence of asthma so high? Why are so many of our students and their families unaware of proper management strategies for asthma? What is the best way to keep asthma under control? What factors in our physical environment and our psychological environment contribute to frequency of asthma episodes? Why do we have so many allergens in our air? How do others deal with asthma? How can we publicize proper care methods to those in our school community who do not receive regular medical care?

Research

This project was designed to emulate the goals and to follow many of the procedures and methodologies of the Project-Enhanced Science Learning (PESL) model (Exhibit 3). In this learning-centered model, students are guided to develop skills in building on prior knowledge and experiences to construct new conceptual understandings (Pfister, 1993). The goal of such an approach is to bring the scientific method into the classroom in a more realistic and meaningful way for students. This approach allows students to learn something interesting and valuable, but also to change their conception about themselves and their own

| EXHIBIT 3 | Gladstone Asthma Project Goals |

1. Build Knowledge via Authentic Tasks
   - Mathematical Problem-Solving Skills
   - Using Scientific Method & Practice
2. Develop Research Skills
   - Using On-Line Reference Sources
   - Contacting "Expert" Sources
3. Practice "Hands-On" Skills of Science
   - Creating and Using Tools
4. Strengthen Cooperative Social Skills
   - Working in Collaborative Groups
   - Conducting Interviews
   - Developing Questionnaires
5. Refine Communications Skills
   - Writing to Express Ideas
   - Persuasive Speaking
   - Interviewing Techniques
   - Creating Multimedia Presentations
6. Enhance Thinking Skills
   - Analyzing & Synthesizing Information
   - Generating Findings & Recommendations
7. Empower Learners
   - Effecting Quality of Own Life
   - Making a Difference in Other's Lives

Note: Adapted from Project-Enhanced Science Learning (PESL) Model by Gladstone Elementary, 1996.

efficacy (Tinker, 1993). Students become involved learners as they are guided in constructing their own tools as well as in using scientific investigation tools (e.g., water quality assessment devices) to solve relevant problems.

For this project, students will be studying air quality and its relation to incidence of asthma using a simple syringe air pump developed by TERC (Technical Education Research Centers) for school use. TERC, a company based in Massachusetts, develops a variety of educational materials that emulate the tools and methods used by practitioners in the scientific fields. Many of their projects incorporate shared databases of information gathered by students around the world. By following the elements of the TERC model for our investigation of asthma, Gladstone students learn to (a) think like scientists by working with data and addressing substantive problems, (b) collaborate as scientists by working with peers and mentors to plan and carry out an investigation, (c) communicate and debate their findings, and (d) evaluate their own work and the work of others (Feldman & McWilliams, 1995).

Communication technologies will allow Gladstone students to collaborate with others in different environments. By sharing and comparing their data, students will build knowledge and develop increased confidence in their own abilities. Through connection with the TERC program, as well as over the Internet in general, students will have direct access to a rich set of resources on-line, including scientists and health-care experts, for information gathering and discussion of their hypotheses and ideas. Students will be learning multimedia techniques and new communication skills for sharing information as they present their ideas and information to a broad audience in a persuasive and useful manner.

Broad Student Outcomes

Many of the Gladstone project outcomes relate to Illinois State Goals as well as our local curricular expectations for sixth grade. In Science, students will be able to

◻ recognize relationships between science and technology and the social and environmental implications and limitations of technological development.

◻ gain a working knowledge of the principles of scientific research and experimentation and apply these in simple research projects as they gather, report, analyze, and communicate data using the process skills of science (observing, classifying, predicting, interpreting data, inferring, concluding, etc.).

In Math, students will be able to

◻ understand and use methods of data collection and analysis, including charts, tables and comparisons.

□ make and use measurements, including those of area and volume.

□ use mathematical skills to estimate, approximate, and predict outcomes and to judge reasonableness of results.

In Physical Development and Health, students will be able to

□ understand the principles of nutrition, exercise, efficient management of emotional stress, positive self-concept development, drug use and abuse, and the prevention and treatment of illness.

□ understand consumer health and safety, including environmental health.

In Language Arts, students will be able to

□ read, comprehend, interpret, evaluate and use written material.

□ listen critically and analytically.

□ use spoken language effectively in formal and informal situations to communicate ideas and information and to ask and answer questions.

Students will also be developing outcome skills of the sixth grade social studies curriculum as they share and compare their results with those of students from other areas, noting not only the differences but similarities between the groups. In the process, students will also learn to use various information and communication technologies, to communicate their needs to community leaders and policy makers, and to be an educated consumer of the available health-care systems.

Broad Task and Ill-Structured Problem or Question

Students will engage in investigations to gather information related to the overarching question of this study: "Why is there so much asthma in our community and what can we do about it?" Over the course of this project, students will build and refine a common knowledge base related to the various causes and triggers, rates of incidence, means of prevention, and effective treatments of asthma. The class will collaboratively establish a set of findings and recommendations that can then be shared with interested and authentic audiences (i.e., those who might also benefit) within and beyond the school community.

Assessment

One of the key outcomes of this project will be an increase in our students' sense of responsibility for and feelings of efficacy related to maintaining their own health as well as that of others within their community. Assessment will be performance-based and ongoing throughout the project. There will be an opportunity for each student group to present their findings and recommendations to an authentic audience, either from within the local community or beyond. Presentations may be in the form of writing, video, persuasive speaking with visual aids, hypermedia (computer-supported multimedia), or other appropriate format determined by students and their teachers. Students and teachers will codevelop criteria for acceptable and exemplary performance and mastery of outcomes. Students will also submit artifacts and interim summaries of their work to be collected in a class binder for this project. Additionally, students may elect to keep a reflective journal of their work to be shared with another student or one of their teachers.

FLOW OF THE PROJECT AND TIMELINE

This unit of study will continue for one trimester or approximately 12 weeks. As part of this project, Gladstone plans to join TERC's Global Lab Network, which introduces students to real-world science. Through this program, students acquire research experience while they learn essential technical skills and scientific method via high interest, hands-on activities in the classroom. The core philosophy of the Global Lab is to teach basic investigative skills, methodologies, and scientific ethics to students before they undertake advanced research projects. So, prior to beginning the 6-week group investigative phase, we will have spent another 6 weeks of class time developing skill in the basics of scientific method and of collecting and analyzing data using the Global Lab curricular materials. Use of these materials and practice projects will allow a knowledge base to develop that can then be applied during the problem-based study of asthma.

The flow of this project will be organized around a number of student research groups, each group focusing on a separate problem related to the question, "Why is there so much asthma in our community and what can we do about it?" Initially, this broad task and problem will be presented to students by sharing anecdotal incidents that convey the importance and relevance of this upcoming unit. Teachers will guide students in developing a preliminary concept map, which will help define problem areas to consider in answering the broad question. We plan to use a management template developed by the authors of this book to organize the flow of group work. We found it useful in our preliminary planning to speculate how the scope of this unit might play out with potential student groups (see Figure 6).

Students will work in small, self-selected groups, gathering information and formulating answers to guiding questions. Each "expert" group will determine their own question for inquiry related to cause and impact, rates of incidence, means of prevention, and effective treatments based on these aspects of asthma as a disease: physical, so-cial-demographic, psychological, and environmental. Over the course of this project, students will build and refine a common knowledge base related to the various aspects of asthma. Throughout this project, we want all students to achieve each of the identified outcomes for science, math, health, language arts, and social studies. All groups will employ the scientific method in their study as they establish findings and recommendations. Students will also be expected to share their work not only with their classmates, but with another group of peers or adult mentors on-line.

PBL Unit: | **Timeframe:** 6 WEEKS | **Teacher(s):** DELANIE & PAUL

Class Broad Task(s) and Problem(s):

* EVERYONE SHOULD FOCUS ON: WHY SO MUCH ASTHMA / WHAT TO DO ABOUT IT?

	Group Name: Students:	Group Name: Students:	Group Name: Students:	Group Name: Students:	Group Name: Students:
	• RATE OF INCIDENCE? • CAUSES, TRIGGERS, IMPACT? • PREVENTION? • TREATMENT/ MANAGEMENT?				
Group Problem/ Question	KIDS WILL — PHYSICAL ASPECTS	DEVELOP QUESTIONS/ SOCIAL/ DEMOGRAPHIC FACTORS	PROBLEMS FOR PSYCHOLOGICAL FACTORS	THESE AREAS/FACTORS * ENVIRONMENTAL FACTORS	OTHER FACTORS
Primary Resources & Sites	• CENTERS FOR DISEASE CONTROL • HEALTH DEPARTMENTS & AGENCIES • LOCAL MEDICAL CENTERS • NURSING CENTER			• TERC • LOCAL UNIVERSITIES? • INTERNET • OTHER SCHOOLS . WHAT ELSE?	
Presentations & Products	(KIDS SHOULD HAVE LOTS OF IDEAS ...) - VIDEO FOR FAMILIES? - PRESENT TO SCHOOL COUNCIL W/ RECOMMENDATIONS? - HOMEPAGE FOR KIDS W/ASTHMA? - NEWSPAPER COVERAGE?				
Authentic Audiences	TAP INTO REPRESENTATIVES FROM RESOURCES FOR AUDIENCE PLUS — COMMUNITY MEMBERS WITH ASTHMA OR W/IN FAMILY — SCHOOL COMMUNITY WITH ASTHMA OR W/IN FAMILY				

Figure 6 PBL-CD management template: Small group monitoring record.

It will be especially empowering for students to formulate and modify guiding questions as they conduct their own investigations, analyze research conducted by others, and generate solutions to a real problem. Throughout this project, students will convene as a single group to share findings and ideas, working together toward consolidating and synthesizing the growing pool of information about asthma. Teachers, and possibly outside experts, will ask probing and guiding questions to assist students in bringing the concepts and ideas into clear focus. As this debriefing process continues, it will be easier for students to make recommendations that incorporate all aspects of the problem of managing and preventing asthma within a community.

During the course of this trimester-long project, students will develop research skills by accessing current data related to the cause and treatment of asthma. They will go on-line to search for appropriate and useful material and to consult professionals in the field. Gladstone is fortunate to have on-line capacity in both the learning center and in the science room. Although our infrastructure does not currently allow a "robust" connection (capable of full-motion video and speedy retrieval of graphics), we do have graphical interface connection to the Internet. We hope that in subsequent years of using this unit our telecommunications capacity will be improved.

Groups of students will construct and post on-line their own questionnaire related to asthma for other students and professionals to complete. Information will be entered into a database for a variety of mathematical analysis activities.

Students will learn to use the TERC simple air pump to gather samples from a variety of locations in their environment. Data collected on air quality will also be entered into a database for analysis and the results will be graphed for comparison. Students will compare the local incidence rate of asthma and students' current management methods with data gathered from health-related sources, such as the Center for Disease Control, and from questions asked of students at other schools. Students will devise various means of reporting and presenting a synthesis of their findings and recommendations according to the needs of a variety of audiences—peers, older or younger siblings, teachers and school personnel, parents and family members of asthmatics, community members, policy makers, or medical practitioners. Final presentations will be based on small group investigations as well as the whole group consolidation of research related to treatment and prevention for the areas of physical, social-demographic, psychological, and environmental concerns.

A final series of debriefings will occur after each of the group presentations to review the process and make any adjustments to the class concept map. Ideas for further study might also be generated at this time.

SAMPLE ACTIVITIES

This unit may generate a great variety of activities. One activity we will do is to use the scientific method to see what elements in the environment are affecting the students' asthma. The procedure will be as follows:

1. Students will collect air samples from the environments frequented by the students. They will use a hand-drawn syringe air pump, designed by TERC for school-use. Although simple, the pump is accurate in collecting air to be analyzed.

2. The air samples will be analyzed using scientific protocols from the PESL (project-enhanced science learning) methodology.

3. Students will plot and graph data, and create a database of pertinent information to be shared with other schools on-line.

4. The results will form a basis for class discussions. Students will have opportunities to compare data with students from other demographic backgrounds by communicating on-line with students from schools in the suburbs or across the country. Through this knowledge sharing between schools in different locations, we will see if there is a correlation between the environment and the incidence

of asthma episodes. Students will learn what allergens trigger their individual episodes and where these allergens are found in their environment (with the air analyzer). With this information and using results from the group investigations, students can learn how to eliminate as many allergens as possible, making a healthier environment for themselves and their classmates.

In another activity, nursing students from the Family Nursing Center will work with Gladstone students to develop a working knowledge of respiratory anatomy and physiology as well as on the pathophysiology of asthma. Students will be coached in using a simple tool called a peak flow meter to measure the velocity of their exhalation (which detects early stages of airway obstruction) at rest, after exercise; and for those students with asthma, during an episode both before and after using an inhaler. Students will then graph and analyze this data with their classmates. They will compare the peak air flow of those children who do not have asthma with those who do. Students will keep a journal for 2 to 3 weeks documenting such things as the weather, stress, exercise, and the resulting effects on their own respiration. By also publishing their data on-line, students can also compare their results with those from other schools of different demographic characteristics.

REFLECTION AND SELF-ASSESSMENT

This unit has not yet been taught and can therefore not be evaluated. It may be helpful to formulate a few reflective points to consider and questions to guide ongoing evaluation and refinement of this unit as it is used with students.

For example, we want to make sure that this truly is an authentic and relevant task for students. We anticipate that they will have a vested interest in their learning related to asthma, their environment, and development and maintenance of sound heath-care practices. Clues to us as teachers in this project will be to monitor the informal conversation and reporting of findings of students—are they excited enough to want to regularly update their classmates and families at home?

We will also want to assess the management issues of accomplishing our goals and achieving the identified student outcomes. Are the tasks and roles assumed by students broad enough to cover a range of concepts, yet narrow enough so as not to lose impact and accessibility to specific skills? What have our students learned about building knowledge through sharing and refining their findings? Do the performance-based assessments reflect the students' highest level of learning, or are they more for show than substance?

Most importantly, we want to assess whether our students truly have been involved in a codevelopment process. Have they been provided sufficient opportunities to contribute to the evolving activities of this unit? If not, where do we need to make changes for future uses of this unit?

We have made an effort to follow the design process for problem-based learning offered in this book and have found the process to be workable. We feel that all of the elements were considered in the planning process, so we anticipate that the classroom implementation of this project should go quite well. We are hopeful that the learning experience will be a powerful one, not only for our students and the school community, but for us as learners, too.

A MUSEUM PROJECT: PARALLEL EVOLUTION

Shella Schlaggar and Gail Sims Smith, *Edison Regional Gifted Center*

Overview of the Project

Ours is an interdisciplinary project involving three classrooms, one each from grades four, five, and six, in a 6-week study of parallel evolution. The project initially linked our students with partners at the Brookfield Zoo near Chicago in the study of the physical structures and adaptations for survival of toucans and hornbills, as well as the environment in which each species lives. Math skills were enhanced as data were gathered and analyzed. A study of geography, climate, and the ecosystem of the birds' ranges allowed for conclusions and projections. Students utilized reference skills, both at the school and over the Internet to research the available materials on their topics. The final aspect of the project was museum-quality exhibits that detailed the two types of birds and their habitats and compared and contrasted the niche occupied by each bird. The display highlighted the plight of the rain forest and documented student conclusions as to why there are species or types of animals in one part of the world similar to animals in another.

This project was planned in the Fall of 1994 and taught in the Spring of 1995. It will be taught again, building on the feedback and analysis of the first cycle.

DESCRIPTION OF THE SCHOOL

The Edison Regional Gifted Center is a Chicago Public School serving 275 students in kindergarten through eighth grades identified as academically gifted. Our students have been selected through an approved process, according to federal and state guidelines. As part of a desegregation initiative, our students represent the cultural, ethnic, and socio-economic diversity of our urban setting: 36% White, 13% African American, 22% Asian, 25% Hispanic, and 5% Native American. They are bused from a wide geographic area of the city. Edison is a small school with one class per grade, with a fairly informal, intimate environment where students are able to exercise personal initiative and to act on their self-motivation.

Our learning resource center is well-equipped with standard school research materials and a good computer lab. Classroom materials are also plentiful. Our use of technology is expanding; but during the first year of this project, it was at a very basic level—CD-ROM research, word-processing, graphics, and video. The school is now ready for voice, video, and data connectivity (i.e., the ability to access resources within and beyond the school because of connections to those resources).

In terms of educational philosophy, we believe in an experiential, hands-on approach that is oriented towards specific goals. We want students to be able to demonstrate their knowledge and understanding through application and construction. It is our belief that students should be both consumers and producers of knowledge.

The faculty, under the direction of Sheila Schlaggar, the principal, has moved away from textbook-based instruction toward problem-focused, project-based instruction, employing inquiry and scientific method applications across content areas, multiple resources, model-building, and performance and portfolio assessments. During the past 3 years, faculty stability has been an issue because of early retirement opportunities. However, although half of the faculty is new to the school, with the leadership of the principal and Gail Smith, librarian and technology-media specialist, the movement to implement problem- and project-based learning and to use technology to enhance learning continues to grow and strengthen the instructional program.

The lead teacher for the Museum Project was Jack Matsumoto, a science teacher. Another science teacher, three homeroom teachers, and a student teacher joined Jack, Gail, and Sheila in guiding, planning, and implementing the unit.

RATIONALE FOR THE PROJECT

Purposes

We saw problem-based learning as a natural extension of our school's strong science instruction and of our movement toward a more integrated, inquiry-oriented program. We recognized that authentic learning took place if students were involved in meaningful activities valued by others. We stressed multiple intelligences and students' personal development of their intelligences. We envisioned this project to be an integration of those qualities of learning.

We selected biology for our major content area, and focused on a parallel evolution question relating to the development of two similar birds, hornbills and toucans. We investigated their physical structures, places in their ecosystems, and adaptations for survival. The study of geography, climate, habitat, plants and animals of the birds' respective ecosystems, research skills, mathematics for the organization of data, reading, writing, arts and crafts, and the use of technology were important to the facilitation of the project.

Research

Our research base was twofold: (a) the twin metaphor of museum-as-school and school-as-museum, and (b) the role of multiple intelligences. We chose the museum idea from Gardner's book, *The Unschooled Mind: How Children Think and How Schools Should Teach* (1991), to drive the vision for our project. In his book, he argues that classroom learning should be more like learning in museums: that is, a more informal atmosphere involving hands-on experience with materials, whereby learning is more spontaneous and involves many aspects of thinking. Looking at the other side of the metaphor, we knew that museums, zoos, and other sites of informal learning, were becoming increasingly interested in reaching out to schools, not only to work with them but also to have exhibits in schools. As it turned out, we had an interest in working with museums. Putting these ideas together, we thought that making some displays for our school and for the Brookfield Zoo would be an authentic task, especially if we had input from the zoo along the way.

We wanted to stress the role of the multiple intelligences (MI) model in designing and developing the overall project. We had experimented with embedding selected pieces of Gardner's theory in less ambitious activities. We thought that the notions of individual learning styles, preferences, and perspectives lent themselves very well to a broad-based undertaking. We saw the great span of individual differences within our student population, especially in the grades targeted for this project. Our students often seemed to be pushing themselves, trying to find out about their strengths and weaknesses. What we wanted to do was to provide choices, to encourage more than verbal-linguistic or logical-mathematical abilities, to help students see that learning is a multidimensional process.

Another significant factor, clearly grounded in the multidimensional process, is the natural relationship of learning to ability and interest rather than an artificial connection to age or grade. We wanted to further expand the students' possibilities by blending the cross-graded structure with the MI structure.

From our previous MI efforts, we had come to realize the complexity of its format. Its complexity is related to the manner in which the MI lesson format needs to be integrated into the instructional process. We knew that we had to design those types of lessons, directly relating them to the Museum Project. We believed that the students' knowledge of their intelligences, ability to utilize their intelligences, and knowledge of what their intelligences could do for them would be our actual goal, with the Museum Project as the means with which to accomplish it.

Broad Task and Problem

The driving question for the Museum Project was: How is it that two similar birds, toucans and hornbills, developed and live in two different parts of the world? The initial broad task was twofold: (a) students were to do research to address this question and (b) they were to build a museum exhibit that would be on display at the Brookfield Zoo. The assumption was that the exhibit would focus on telling the story of the parallel evolution of the two birds.

Student Outcomes and Assessments

The student requirements for the project were on two levels. On the first level, students worked within their class in groups and kept research notes and illustrations, prepared a fact sheet on a self-selected topic, created a visual, constructed an artifact from one of the ecosystems, wrote an informational piece for a text, organized personal research in order to teach and inform others, and prepared a talk on a self-selected topic from personal research. On the second level, students worked in cross-graded groups and shared their personal research, produced a brochure for zoo, community, and school patrons, created a segment of the physical exhibit, completed a paper and pencil test on the material studied, prepared to act as docents for tours and invited guests, and responded to an evaluation assessment of the entire project. Nearly all of the artifacts or products of student work throughout the project were evaluated using teacher- or student-developed assessments.

Although we had specific requirements and assessments, we also realized that for students' optimum success we needed to allow for student self-direction, cooperative decision making, and creative expression. We found ourselves constantly talking through what we were doing: checking to see that the basics were covered and that the basic skills were combined with evolving, increasingly complex skills. This skill-building process increased the meaning and value of what the students were designing, creating, and producing.

FLOW OF THE PROJECT AND EXAMPLES OF ACTIVITIES

When we began the Museum Project, we realized that it was going to be an expanding experience. Figure 7 shows the flow of the project, as planned for, over a six week period. Both the teachers and the students felt the need for more overall direction in what was expected and what could be done. They wanted to see what an exhibit would look like. We took the students to a local city zoo and to a natural history museum, prepared to see what an actual museum project or exhibit looked like and ready to analyze its component parts. Museum and zoo personnel met with us and came to Edison to work with students. We also visited the main city library for better access to research information. The science librarian was very helpful and continued to provide information throughout the project.

Soon it also became apparent that students' interests and questioning would influence our direction. We watched the students take-off and drive the project. Their passionate concern about the plight of the rainforest as an environment became the driving force for the exhibit,

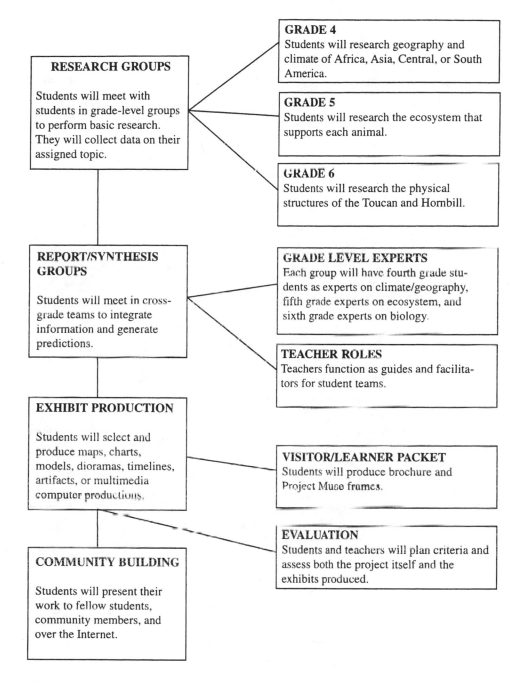

RESEARCH GROUPS

Students will meet with students in grade-level groups to perform basic research. They will collect data on their assigned topic.

GRADE 4
Students will research geography and climate of Africa, Asia, Central, or South America.

GRADE 5
Students will research the ecosystem that supports each animal.

GRADE 6
Students will research the physical structures of the Toucan and Hornbill.

REPORT/SYNTHESIS GROUPS

Students will meet in cross-grade teams to integrate information and generate predictions.

GRADE LEVEL EXPERTS
Each group will have fourth grade students as experts on climate/geography, fifth grade experts on ecosystem, and sixth grade experts on biology.

TEACHER ROLES
Teachers function as guides and facilitators for student teams.

EXHIBIT PRODUCTION

Students will select and produce maps, charts, models, dioramas, timelines, artifacts, or multimedia computer productions.

VISITOR/LEARNER PACKET
Students will produce brochure and Project Muse frames.

EVALUATION
Students and teachers will plan criteria and assess both the project itself and the exhibits produced.

COMMUNITY BUILDING

Students will present their work to fellow students, community members, and over the Internet.

Figure 7 *Flow chart for Museum Project. Copyright Gail Sims Smith, 1995. Used by permission.*

rather than the original research question about the two birds.

Specifically, the students' projects grew from a simple, straightforward walk-by exhibit highlighting two birds and their habitats to a complex, three-dimensional walk-through exhibit emphasizing the plight of the rainforest as an environment. Almost every day, science teacher Jack Matsumoto came up with an alteration either the students, other teachers, or he had devised. The addition of lighting, small reptiles and amphibians, fish, papier-mâché trees, a photo scrapbook or journal, background music, and a student-made videotape escalated the enthusiasm. The teachers became more interactive and less directive; they worked side-by-side with students, promoting opportunities for exercising initiative, creativity, and responsibility. Students and teachers could be seen as exchanging roles and teaching each other. This was especially apparent during the tours.

The students focused their energy and enthusiasm on their school exhibit rather than on the zoo exhibit. So, we invited museum, zoo, library, and university personnel, school officials, parents, one of the PBL codevelopers, and schoolmates to tour the school exhibit. Every cross-grade group prepared its own presentation, each student acting first as a part of the group and then one-on-one with guests and visitors. Having real audiences made a difference: Watching the interactions, we actually witnessed the students' realization that they had learned some powerful material and that their work was important and valuable to others. It was electric! We saw that the learning process continued and that new knowledge was being created. The students' respect for their work, for themselves, and for each other was clearly obvious. Students who had never taken responsibility for work, did so.

The students substantiated these observations when describing their experiences and insights into their learning in the project evaluation instrument that they later completed. Another especially gratifying and unexpected student revelation was that they recognized value and potential in the cross-graded structure. They were able to articulate their appreciation for the opportunity to work and learn with others.

REFLECTIONS ON THE UNIT AND PROJECTIONS FOR RETEACHING

Integrating the daily lessons, the materials, the emerging stages of intelligences of the MI model, the three classes, and the evolving construction of the artifacts and exhibit pieces, all on schedule, was an on-going challenge. We learned a lot.

We used every bit of on-site resources available. Students and teachers found themselves gathering data, materials, and even people from outside the school during the project. Parents brought in personal items, even pets, to share with us. The fourth through sixth grade classroom walls were plastered with photos and illustrations of the two birds and their rainforest habitats. The Learning Resource Center (LRC) was inundated with students, paper, texts, and software. Teachers and students brought and used a variety of materials, commercial and school, to do the physical creation and construction of the exhibit.

We reorganized parts of the school day to arrange time for students and faculty to work together. Everybody gave extra personal time to guarantee the successful completion of the project. Some things were unanticipated and required last minute planning time. The LRC teacher, Gail Smith, found herself rescheduling the Flex and Open Lab time in order to accommodate the heavy demand.

We know now that we must expand our resources for our second year. We also know that we must provide an alternative schedule for the rest of the school during this period so that the other students and teachers will be involved in equally meaningful, productive, and fun projects.

Because the students were more interested in focusing their efforts on the environmental issues and problems related to the rainforest than they did on the hornbill and the toucan, the project's academic goals were incomplete. We will redesign what we did as the basis for the next exhibit. We will create the new Museum Project by building upon the knowledge and the database that the students generated this year, making it more of a progressive problem-solving effort. When reteaching this unit, we want our students to be able to

- concentrate on the evolution of the birds within their ecosystems, studying the similarities and differences in their physical structures that make it possible for the individual birds to survive in that ecosystem.

- speculate on the birds' survival in their changing ecosystems, analyzing what they need to survive.

- predict survival rates in an artificial ecosystem constructed in the future—on earth, in space, or on another planet—selecting and describing that ecosystem.

We will consider this only as a framework, allowing students to construct their own research questions, opportunities and applications.

In rethinking our unit, we are considering many other changes. Increasing the numbers of groups will mean smaller numbers in each group (8-9). Increasing the numbers of faculty and other adults will mean greater guidance. Increasing the amount of advance planning will clarify roles and responsibilities. Putting clear criteria for completion of each piece of the exhibit will lend itself to evaluation. Setting a specific timeline with expectations of finished items will aid in the collection of data on learning at each level of the project. Having technology and internet connectivity in place will expand research capabilities. Building additional museum and community partnerships will broaden student experiences. Finding more durable construction materials will mean a more lasting set of artifacts and construction of the display. Identifying roles and responsibilities within grade level and across grade level groups will make the cooperative learning experience more effective and efficient.

Technology will be an increasingly integral part of the production of the next Museum Project exhibit. After the project was completed, we were able to make some new connections to outside resources. Networking with the Museum, Zoo, Argonne National Laboratory, and AT&T began immediately. Sheila connected with the educational director of the city aquarium to further the aquatic piece of the rainforest ecosystem. Jack spent a week at the Smithsonian, learning about the breadth and depth of the national resources at our disposal electronically. He also learned how to access those resources using technology and how to use technology to integrate art into the curriculum. Some discussion has taken place regarding a home page, electronic dialogue with research scientists in the field, as well as communication and exchange with students and teachers in other schools.

We also want to follow up on the potential for sharing the exhibit with other schools and for having it showcased at a "real" museum or library. Because we are "seasoned" veterans, we have some experience to draw upon from the technical aspects as well as the instructional ones. We know that we cannot anticipate the storehouse of ideas that the students will generate, but we have a clearer picture of the possibilities for the display. So much conversation was sparked by the variety of constructed pieces, the style of the brochures, the video, and other individual touches, that we are prepared for a veritable explosion in next year's creativity.

Finally, we are committed to continuing the multiple intelligences model. Figure 8 shows how we now conceptualize the seven intelligences in our two student roles: student as consumer of knowledge and student as producer of knowledge.

We witnessed the empowerment and self-actualization of our children as learners and teachers, as consumers and producers of knowledge. We have also strengthened ourselves as teachers and learners, conduits for increasing opportunities. We will be watching and studying our students as they respond to these opportunities and take the project to the next step. We will be watching them to see what they are able to do with what they are learning, as they face complex problem-solving and they create solutions. We want to find new and more meaningful ways to record, document, and evaluate what the students and the project achieve. We look forward to implementing our work in the next school year.

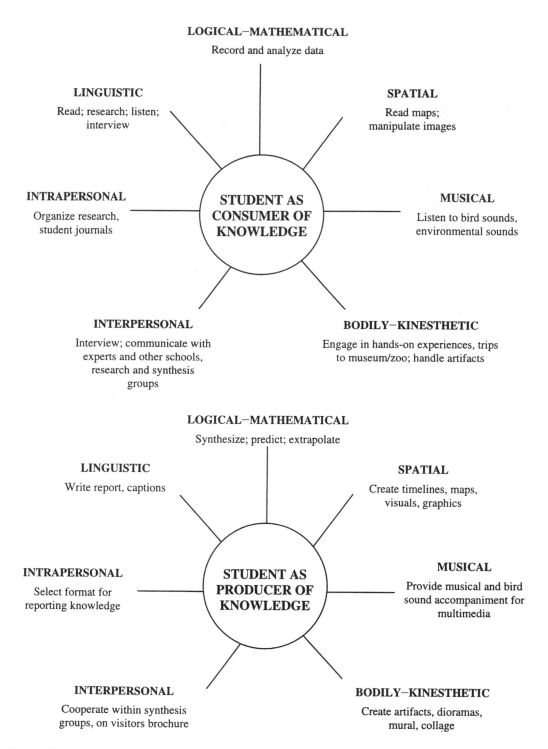

LOGICAL–MATHEMATICAL
Record and analyze data

LINGUISTIC
Read; research; listen;
interview

SPATIAL
Read maps;
manipulate images

INTRAPERSONAL
Organize research,
student journals

STUDENT AS
CONSUMER OF
KNOWLEDGE

MUSICAL
Listen to bird sounds,
environmental sounds

INTERPERSONAL
Interview; communicate with
experts and other schools,
research and synthesis
groups

BODILY–KINESTHETIC
Engage in hands-on experiences, trips
to museum/zoo; handle artifacts

LOGICAL–MATHEMATICAL
Synthesize; predict; extrapolate

LINGUISTIC
Write report, captions

SPATIAL
Create timelines, maps,
visuals, graphics

INTRAPERSONAL
Select format for
reporting knowledge

STUDENT AS
PRODUCER OF
KNOWLEDGE

MUSICAL
Provide musical and bird
sound accompaniment for
multimedia

INTERPERSONAL
Cooperate within synthesis
groups, on visitors brochure

BODILY–KINESTHETIC
Create artifacts, dioramas,
mural, collage

Figure 8 *Multiple intelligences and student roles. Copyright Gail Sims Smith, 1995. Used by permission.*

In this activity, we will focus on *Phase 2: Developing a Plan of Inquiry and Work*

1a **Understanding the Teacher Authors' PBL-CD Units:** Compare and contrast ideas from the two PBL-CD units. What useful ideas have these teacher authors incorporated into their PBL-CD units? Which ideas are unique to each unit and which are common to both units? Record them in the appropriate areas of this Venn diagram:

What Can We Do About Asthma   A Museum Project:
in Our Community?   Parallel Evolution

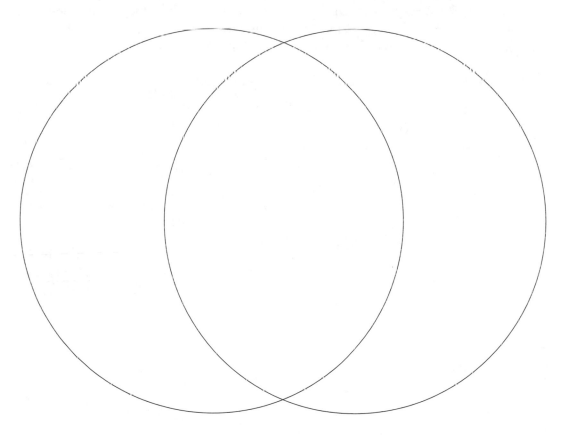

1b **Understanding and Planning for Your PBL-CD Units:** *Phase 2—Developing a Plan of Inquiry and Work.* Using Goal 3 and Appendix C as references, what ideas from the Venn diagram would be most useful to you as you build upon plans in preparation for Phase 2?

Think about how these ideas and ideas from earlier units will help you to prepare for Phase 2 of progressive problem solving in the classroom: What teaching and learning strategies will help you and your students identify specific problems? What teacher roles and student roles will be most appropriate throughout this phase?

Teacher Roles	Teaching Goals and Strategies	Student Roles	Learning Strategies and Responsibilities

2

Acting and Sharing: When you have completed a draft of possible instructional activities for Phase 2, share your ideas with a critical friend team. Describe your plans for your informal conference below.

Process for a critical friend dialogue:

◻ share your desired outcome for the conversation
◻ ask your critical friend to practice active listening and ask clarifying questions
◻ offer constructive, nonjudgmental feedback

3

Reflecting: Reflect upon the outcomes of your critical friend conference. List or in some way represent them (metaphor, graphic organizer, icon).

Rethinking and Refining: What are the implications for you or your team's unit plan?

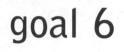

goal 6

Applying PBL-CD to Interdisciplinary
Multicultural Studies

The two Profiles in this Goal provide contrasting approaches to interdisciplinary multicultural studies. The first was developed by a teacher author team from Whittier Elementary School in Chicago, a school with an almost entirely Hispanic student body. The second unit was taught at the Marie Murphy Junior High in Avoca, Illinois, a relatively heterogeneous suburban school population: Although most students are White, there are many Asian cultures represented and those students who are not Asian represent diverse European and Mediterranean cultures. These projects reflect the differing backgrounds of the students of each school, as well as different approaches to PBL-CD.

In the first Profile, the teachers focus on celebrating the students' cultural heritage through "The Aztec Study: Building on Children's Capital by Exploring Our Aztec Past." Although social studies is clearly the lead subject area, the project also involves elements of both science and mathematics. The research base here is interesting not only for its appropriateness for the learning context but also for its authenticity for the teachers at Whittier. Kolian, the lead author, did her Masters' research on the work of Louis Moll. Moll's constructivist approach, emphasizing that all persons represent funds of knowledge and human capital, offers a rich perspective for multicultural approaches in the classroom, but is little known among teachers generally. This Profile greatly enriches our knowledge base on this topic and provides a viable approach for any school wishing to honor the cultural heritage of its students. This unit has already been taught, and there are plans to reteach it in an enhanced form indicated in the "Reflections" section. This unit shows the struggle that teachers have between the need to explore their own limits and those of their students and the need for accountability in the management of small group work and in the assessment of social and academic skills.

Rasmussen and her colleagues provide a rich approach for a different learning context. The student population at Marie Murphy Junior High represents diverse European, Mediterranean, and Asian cultures. Whereas the Aztec unit was exploratory in nature, "Reflecting the World Around Us: Building Multicultural Understanding" was highly sequenced and plotted conceptually before its inception. Whereas the Whittier unit defined authenticity in terms of the meaningfulness of the cultural focus and the authentic audience (display of artifacts in the schools' museum area), the Avoca unit is essentially a simulation that requires students to work through intellectually the various roles for a student election, an event of major consequence in their lives.

THE AZTEC STUDY: BUILDING ON CHILDREN'S CAPITAL BY EXPLORING OUR AZTEC PAST

Susan Kolian, Kim Alamar, and Sheila Epstein, *Whittier Elementary School*

Overview of the Project

The purpose of The Aztec Study was to integrate our students' cultural background into the curriculum in order to provide a context for learning that enhances both their academic performance and their personal and cultural identity. The 8-week unit involved students from two fourth grade bilingual classrooms in a multidisciplinary investigation of MesoAmerican history. Children began the unit by building their knowledge of the Aztec civilization through story telling, videos, and hands-on activities. Working collaboratively in small groups, children shared their knowledge and engaged in learning tasks that facilitated development of bilingual skills in math, social studies, geography, science, and the language arts. Then the children used higher order thinking skills in order to examine the effects of the Spanish invasion of Mexico. We capitalized on the students' own experiences of present day Mexico throughout the unit. Children were often challenged to compare their lives in Mexico with the lives of their ancestors, the Aztecs.

The students' understanding of the topic was further enhanced through group projects that required students to create artifacts of their choice that represented various aspects of Aztec life and the colonization of Mexico by the Spaniards. The students had to demonstrate and share the knowledge gained from their group work by giving presentations using their artifacts and the results of their research. Finally, students designed and provided informational tours of an exhibition composed of the artifacts from their group projects.

DESCRIPTION OF SCHOOL

John Greenleaf Whittier Elementary School (or La Escuela Whittier, as it is known by our families) is a neighborhood school located in the heart of Pilsen, a Near Southeast community in the city of Chicago. For over a 100 years, this area has been a port of entry for waves of immigrants, most of whom came to America from war-torn European nations after World War II and, more recently, from economically depleted Latin American countries. Currently, we serve students ages 3 through 13, and operate Head Start through the sixth grade. Out of the 553 students we serve, approximately 172 were born in Mexico, whereas the remaining are of Mexican American background. Also, 87% of our children live in homes of limited economic resources and come from families whose income falls in the lower indexes of the socioeconomic scale.

Whittier School is committed to honoring the rich cultural heritage that our families have brought with them from their homeland. Within the past 2 years, teachers and staff members, guided by the Local School Council and the Professional Personnel Advisory Committee, have embarked on an effort to transform our ways of teaching and learning. This school-wide reform is driven by a vision of learning founded on principals of problem-based learning, dual language acquisition, and technology for engaged learning. In an attempt to adhere to these principals of reform instruction, we developed The Aztec Study unit.

The Aztec Study was developed by Susan Kolian, a bilingual resource teacher, and Kim Alamar and Sheila Epstein, mainstream classroom teachers. Collaborative planning and teaching of the project was made possible through our work together as a "pod." (At Whittier, pods are small groups of grade level teachers that consist of two mainstream classroom teachers and one bilingual teacher.) Together, we have made a major commitment to providing a culturally appropriate, dual language learning environment in our classrooms. Although authentic learning tasks have always been an integral part of teaching and learning in our classrooms, we are in the beginning stages of fully understanding and implementing problem-based learning. In fact, The Aztec Study began as an open-ended, exploratory unit, and over the 8-week period it began to develop to have characteristics of problem-based learning.

RATIONALE, PURPOSE, AND RESEARCH BASE

In their quest for a better life, many of our students' families at Whittier immigrated to this country from Mexico. They carried with them hopes that education can change their lives as well as the lives of their kids. However, during their adjustment, our students and their families have faced demands for conformity with new cultural codes and beliefs and endured hardships resulting from miscommunication, stress, and racism. Not surprisingly, our students often experience conflicts in their transition from the home to the school culture. The difficulties children experience in overcoming these cultural barriers sometimes lead them to feel alienated, making them less likely to participate actively in their learning.

Unfortunately, our students are among the increasing numbers of language minority students who have a persistent, high rate of educational failure. This makes them one of the most problematic groups for educators. Students from non-English backgrounds drop out at nearly twice the rate of students from an English language background (Steinberg, Blinde, & Chan, 1982). Part of the problem stems from the overwhelming pressure to make second language learners fluent in English at all costs. Learning English, at the expense of not learning other content areas, becomes the controlling goal of instruction for these students, even if it places them at risk academically.

Too often, educators assume that a child's level of oral proficiency in English indicates a similar level of proficiency in reading and writing of English. As a result, there is a tendency to reduce the curriculum's level of complexity to match the student's level of oral proficiency. Thus, these children who are competent academically in their first language are relegated to very low-level English reading lessons. In short, Latino students are frequently locked into lower levels of curriculum centered on drill and practice, rather than engaged in problem-based learning.

Research has documented the importance of selecting a level of instruction that engages a child in learning activities that require that child to go beyond what she or he is already capable of doing (see, for example, Graves, 1982; Vygotsky, 1978). According to Vygotsky, for instruction to be effective it must be aimed at a child's proximal level, that is, at a point of future learning that is challenging without being overly frustrating. Further, social interactions or scaffolding within this zone need to be organized to support the child's performance at the proximal level until he or she is able to perform independently. The intellectual skills acquired are directly related to how the child interacts with adults and peers in specific problem-solving environments.

Honoring Our Children's Cultural Capital

Classroom ethnographies have been instructive in understanding the successes and failures in the education of Latino children. These studies have shown that there is a significant relationship between cultural congruency in instruction (in both approach and content) and children's cognitive development and academic achievement. In order to understand contextual clues and the nature of a cognitive task, children must be given the opportunity to capitalize on what they know: that is, their cultural and linguistic backgrounds .

Influenced by Vygotskian psychology and ethnographically based research, Luis C. Moll has developed a research program that integrates school, home, and community social resources to provide Latino children with a learning context that supports and enhances performance (Moll & Greenberg, 1990). The basic premise underlying his work is that the necessary resources, or "funds of knowledge," are available within the children and the community; tapping them will produce significant change in the children's schooling. Within our community, knowledge of agriculture and skill in gardening, car maintenance, and storytelling are among the sources of cultural capital that can be related to learning in school.

The purpose of our project on the history of the Aztecs in Mexico was to create a culturally appropriate learning environment in order to help our children achieve beyond their current levels of development. We also intended to help students acquire high levels of literacy so they could process information and develop their critical thinking skills. We believe that the ability to structure learning tasks and knowledge effectively can best be developed through the native language, and then easily transferred to a second language (Cummins, 1986).

We also believe that students must play an active role in determining the "whats" and "hows" of the learning process. Not only does this enable students to practice decision-making skills, but it also builds on their prior knowledge and their personal resources. Further, we have encouraged students to build on the human resources within their family and community by comparing their lives in contemporary Mexico with the lives of their ancestors, the Aztecs.

The knowledge of students' culture can help teachers make lesson content more accessible and meaningful, prevent stereotypes, and increase teachers' awareness of students' learning potential. We believe that, in order to facilitate the cultural adjustment of children, teachers and students need to learn a great deal more about each other, to understand each other's actual cultural background and previous experiences, and to engage in cooperative activities that guarantee academic success.

Examining Multiple Intelligences

The development of our project was also influenced by Howard Gardner's (1993) concept of multiple intelligences. According to Gardner, there are many ways of looking at a child's intelligence. The emphasis on linguistic and logical-mathematical intelligences appears to be the major focus in American education. Teachers spend the majority of their time assessing, grading, and teaching in those areas. Therefore, the English as a second language (ESL) student who learns in his or her second language experiences numerous hurdles. Applying the concept of multiple intelligences allows children to construct knowledge through a variety of ways (i.e., spatial, bodily-kinesthetic, musical, interpersonal, and intrapersonal) rather than strictly through the means of linguistic and logical-mathematical intelligences. Therefore, two exploratory questions were a part of our unit planning: What if our children could express their knowledge of the Aztecs in any way they chose? What would happen and how would it look?

Because we had a strong commitment to the theories outlined above, we thought this study should engage our children in constructing links between their education and their lives in the past, present, and future. The theme of Aztec history formed part of a larger goal in our year-long curriculum to develop our children's self-identity and cultural pride. Prior to investigating our history, we spent the first several months of the school year exploring ourselves, our families, and our community. We felt that if the children had a deeper understanding of where they come from and where they fit in their contemporary world, they would become motivated and more actively involved in their learning. Ultimately, we wanted to prepare them with the appropriate critical thinking tools to confront and succeed in their future.

STUDENT CONCEPTS, SKILLS, AND OUTCOMES

During The Aztec Study, students investigated the following big concepts: culture, race, ethnicity, civilization, history, rituals, religion, discrimination, colonization, and interdependence between living things and the earth. Students developed skill in

❑ reading and comprehension strategies through literature groups and research.

❑ the writing process (draft, revise, edit, rewrite, and share).

❑ listening and speaking skills through oral presentations and small group discussions.

□ social studies knowledge (geography; countries, states, and cities of the northern and southern hemispheres).

□ collaborative skills based on helpfulness, listening, and participation.

We targeted the following broad outcomes for our children:

□ Self-identity and self-esteem will improve by better understanding their past and culture.

□ Literacy skills in English and Spanish will improve through reading, researching, writing about and presenting on the topic of study.

□ Bicultural (Mexican American) awareness will be strengthened.

□ Problem-solving skill through collaborative learning and small inquiry groups will improve.

BROAD TASK AND PROBLEMS, ASSESSMENT, AND FLOW OF THE PROJECT

The First Phase

We began the Aztec project by introducing our classes to the purpose and content of the unit. To introduce the notion of an authentic audience, we told the students that the artifacts they would create would be part of an exhibition that they would design in our school's museum. Throughout the development of this museum exhibit, the students were to learn through collaborative work groups as well as whole group lessons. Children already well-developed in English, children ready to shift into English, and children who needed the concepts to be taught in their first language, Spanish, were divided into different work groups on the basis of their language abilities. The work groups explored information about the Aztecs through trade books, handouts, a social studies text, storytelling, and videos. Sometimes a work group read multiple copies of certain books, at other times they used a set of teacher-developed research questions (see Sample Activities).

We soon discovered there was a tremendous amount of information, activities, and art work constructed by the students. There was also a growing enthusiasm within our classrooms. Often students asked when the next work group would meet, or they would share how much they loved learning about the Aztecs. The trade books were explored during other times within the day, such as DEAR (Drop Everything And Read, a free reading time), and students often chose to take the books home at night. Wondering what concepts were important to each child, we asked ourselves how the children could demonstrate their own personal knowledge of the Aztecs through specific projects.

The Second Phase

When we did the original planning we did not have an end clearly in sight—we could envision only the early knowledge building phase. We began to realize that we needed general, open-ended questions to guide our project: "How have the contributions of the Aztec civilization affected our lives today? What would life be like in Mexico and in the world if the Spaniards had never conquered Mexico?"

After a couple of weeks, we also began to realize that we could not evaluate this unit and the students' knowledge using a multiple choice test alone. We decided to develop a more comprehensive teacher-generated test to assess the children's knowledge of the material. It included four different parts: (a) multiple choice questions, (b) concept webbing or mapping, (c) an essay question, and (d) a "right angle" question that allows children to explain both their factual knowledge and personal opinion on a particular topic. The test was in English and Spanish.

Rethinking the nature of our paper and pencil test in relationship to what and how our students were learning also prompted us to think more about the culminating project, the museum exhibit. The exhibits would be visual and creative and involve oral sharing of information, so we decided to incorporate into our unit a formal performance-based assessment tool using rubrics. (We had never formally evaluated student projects using rubrics.) The criteria for our assessment included skills for student collaboration, presentation, the audience's role during presentations, as well as criteria for the content of the artifacts themselves. For example, the rubric for collaborative group skills identified key criteria as "good listening skills, very helpful, participated fully."

We envisioned the children continuing their work in collaborative groups creating artifacts and further focusing their study through project work; however, they would also follow criteria from the teacher-generated rubrics. During a class meeting, we explained that they would become teachers, sharing their knowledge as docents of the museum. After brainstorming a list of ideas, the children chose to focus their accumulated knowledge on four projects: (a) aspects of Aztec life including marriage, marketing, and gardening, all depicted by murals; (b) a timeline highlighting significant developments in Aztec civilization and its colonization by the Spaniards; (c) artifacts of cultural life; and (d) a reconstruction of the great city of Tenochtitlán, capital of the Aztec empire.

The first assignment for the collaborative work groups was to assign roles for each member and discuss ways for members to demonstrate their knowledge. After each group decided what they planned to make, they had to discuss how to create their project and what materials were needed. At the beginning of each work time, the students were in charge of setting goals and time limits. The goals were then prioritized and used as a daily work agenda that helped them to stay on task. Teachers emphasized social skills. A daily social skill focus might be "practice your best listening skills, or help your members clean up within four minutes."

After collaborative group work time, we would all sit in a circle and listen to the reporters from each group inform us of problems or progress. Circle time provided a forum for troubleshooting and group reflection. Many problems were project-related. One group that decided to create a three dimensional version of Tenochtitlán out of paper had difficulty with the construction. Other students were able to recommend solutions that were successful. Some of the problems were behavior-related. The circle meetings became a time for our students to explore proactive ways of communicating. For the teachers, it was a time to touch base with each group in a focused manner.

After a few circle meetings with the children, we discovered the rubrics were far too difficult. Our rubrics focused on ideal behaviors and skills, having no room for growth. So we teachers debated about making a change in assessment midway through the unit and decided we needed to rewrite the rubrics. The second form of the collaborative group skills rubric was changed to: *Listening* (1) Few to no listening skills (2) Some listening skills (3) Uses listening skills regularly; *Cooperation* (1) Does not cooperate (2) Cooperates somewhat (3) Cooperates regularly; *Helpfulness* (1) Is not helpful (2) Helps sometimes (3) Very helpful. Parts of the presentation and artifacts rubrics were refined with the children so that they would know about the assessment criteria.

The students began using this language to assess themselves. We would hear students make statements such as "you're not being very helpful" or "I liked how our group cooperated today." As the children began reflecting on the day's events, on their work, and on the work of others, we noticed various transformations in groups. Our students were becoming metacognitive! We realized the importance of metacognition: According to educator Kay Burke, "students need to self-reflect regularly so that they can become adept at monitoring, assessing, and improving their own [work] and their own thinking," (Burke, 1994, p.95).

After the projects were completed, the students began to present their artifacts. They shared their knowledge with other small groups. They were prepared to answer questions and to translate their research from both languages while providing some form of visual artifact. The audience had a set of behavior rubrics to follow: After the presentation, the audience asked questions and offered constructive criticism, noting what was positive about the project, then offering suggestions for improvement. Because the children "taught" to each small group separately, allowing them a total of four times in front of small audiences to practice and refine their presentation, their communication skills improved.

SAMPLE ACTIVITIES

Knowledge Building

One of the main project activities involved 20, teacher-generated research questions used by the students to guide their investigation of the various cultural aspects of Aztec life. The questions lead them to information that related to broad topics, such as family, religion, education, and government. In order to enhance social interaction and collaboration between our Spanish- and English-dominant learners, the questions and literature were made available in both languages. In heterogeneous pairs and small groups, the children worked together to research the questions, translate their responses, and share their results with each other. The information children derived from their investigation provided the basis for further discussion of the major concepts and relevant vocabulary of the unit. These included culture, civilization, history, archeology, market, taxes, and pyramids.

From the start, children were enthusiastic about the literature and material resources. Many children had prior knowledge of the Aztec civilization from previous classes and from experiences living in Mexican cities where many of the Aztec ruins remain (particularly in the *Distrito Federal*, the capital of Mexico). After discovering a large book on the Aztec pyramids and artifacts, one young boy stated, "I wish I could dive into this book and be an Aztec living in these pyramids." Responses such as these were a clear indication to us that by incorporating their cultural background into the curriculum, children were becoming engaged in their learning.

Through our observation of the children's work and class discussion, it became evident that they were gradually acquiring a command of the concepts and vocabulary in both languages. Depending on the language of instruction of each lesson, children were transferring their knowledge of certain terms they had learned from Spanish to English and vice versa.

Understanding and Using Codices

We began our study of the codices by discussing how these hieroglyphics were used by the Aztecs to communicate ideas, concepts, and stories. Then, we compared the codice system with our alphabet by asking, "Why do we communicate with letters and words, instead of pictures?" After examining the different codices and their meanings, children worked in small groups of 4 to 5 students to construct stories with the codices' graphic representations. Using the knowledge gained from the research activity, they began writing a story related to Aztec history. They wrote the story on the bottom of a large sheet of chart paper and on the top of the sheet they drew their story using only the codices. For example, one codice used by the children depicted an eagle sitting on a rock with a serpent in its mouth. Aztec history tells us that this codice represents the story of the founding of Tenochtitlán. The Aztecs were told by their god that they must build their city where they find an eagle on a rock eating a serpent.

After the children finished their work, each group had to interpret in writing each other's stories, using only the codices. Then, each group read their story aloud to discover which group was able to interpret their stories correctly. This was a wonderful opportunity to assess the children's knowledge of the material covered so far in the unit. Working in collaborative, heterogeneous groups, most of the children experienced a sense of success in completing the learning tasks. We believe this can be attributed to allowing the children to construct the meaning of the information through their visual, interpersonal, and artistic skills. Other project activities that required children to apply various intelligences for learning included the reconstruction of an Aztec pueblo, scaling Tenochtitlán to size, gardening Aztec style, creating Aztec artifacts, and creating murals and timelines of Aztec life.

Making Connections: Past and Present

Throughout the project we worked to guide the children in making connections between past and present. The objective was to help build their knowledge of their history or where they come from in order to better understand themselves. One activity that built upon the fund of storytelling was the reading of the Aztec legend of Food Mountain. This legend depicts how the natural elements— wind, rain, sun, and water—affect living things. It teaches the importance of taking care of the earth, which provides human sustenance. This legend embodies many of the spiritual and world views of the Aztecs. Most of our children are from rural and agricultural backgrounds and have a lot of prior or cultural knowledge of weather, plants, animals, and raising crops. During discussion of the legend, children were guided to make connections to their lives in Mexico. Questions such as the following helped to guide discussion: What do we know about the earth? Why is it important to take care of the earth? What do we know about farming? What do plants and crops need to grow? What do we eat today that is made out of corn? Then the children wrote stories on their "histories" in the campo or countryside in Mexico. They wrote about farming with plants, flowers, or animals, as well as pictorial stories based on the legend using the symbols of the Aztec language.

This reading of the legend was reinforced by nonfictional readings of how the Aztecs farmed, what food they grew, and how their cities gardens, city markets, and economic system operated. The barter system used by the Aztecs—trading furs for food or clay pots for clothes—was a major emphasis in this aspect of our studies because markets are still very prevalent in Mexico. Children shared stories of the markets in Mexico from their own point of view.

The students then researched the colonization of the Aztecs by the Spaniards. Students read nonfictional accounts of the colonization and the consequences of the event were analyzed. Questions such as the following were discussed: How do people treat the Indians differently? Why are they treated differently? How does the color of your skin or the shade of darkness affect the way people treat you? Storytelling by one of our Mexican student teachers about Indian children in Mexico helped the children to understand and articulate this discrimination. Then we talked about race and ethnicity living as Mexicans in Chicago.

REFLECTIONS

Making Assessment More Seamless

Upon reflection on the project's development, we found the assessment component to be very instructive. As mentioned earlier, during the first stage of our unit we realized the need to develop a set of criteria to evaluate the children's knowledge through performance-based assessment. We refined those criteria during the course of the unit on the basis of discussions with our students, making them more developmentally appropriate. The assessment also involved further development of our unit of study in relationship to the culminating project of the museum exhibit. So although we did not initially plan on incorporating this assessment component, the decision resulted in making our instruction more seamless in the second stage of the unit.

A weakness in this area was that nearly all of our criteria were teacher-generated. When approaching this project again, we plan to create the rubrics with the students.

Making the Learning Context More Authentic

A major limitation in our learning context was lack of dual-language materials and resources. Consistent with our school's vision of problem-based learning and commitment to technology as a tool for this learning, we plan to enhance our access to bilingual and bicultural resources through the use of telecommunications. We will seek opportunities to work and learn with and about people in other Spanish-speaking countries, cultures, and classrooms via the Internet.

A central value of working with the Internet is that it can support the authentic learning experiences currently being developed in our classrooms. When teachers and students contribute to the information infrastructure by participating in virtual communities and by setting up information services on the networks, the students' learning experiences naturally become more authentic. The learner has a real and responsive audience, and this can be highly motivating. Children who use the Internet in this way are creating and exchanging knowledge, rather than passively receiving someone else's information. This is consistent with our understanding of how children learn—actively, constructively, collaboratively, multisensorially, within a cultural and linguistic context.

Working with the Internet also provides opportunities to establish cross-institutional and cross-cultural partnerships among administrators, university faculty, community, business, labor and political leaders, as well as parents, teachers, and students. When we reteach this unit, we would like to make better use of our community resources by bringing in representatives of the culture, including family members, historians, and museum staff. Online and local partnerships will bring additional resources to our desktops, requiring us to develop a closer relationship between learning and the real-world context of people, problems, and projects, thus creating further contexts for authentic learning.

Realizing Our Purpose

We believe that our vision of learning was very coherent and strong from the beginning of the unit. We wanted our children to be enthused and energized by the content of this unit, and therefore, responsible for their learning. The tasks were very integrative, including many different content areas simultaneously: history, language arts, science, and fine arts. Children worked in small collaborative groups for the majority of their tasks and activities. The rubrics for collaboration and for the creation and presentation of their artifacts helped the children to develop learning strategies such as goal setting, setting agendas, keeping time, and problem-solving.

What really worked was our grouping. Spanish dominant and English dominant children worked side by side. Children were moving from Spanish to English in their knowledge and terminology. We made every attempt possible to keep groups equitable and flexible by never segregating kids according to language or ability.

The teachers could have acted more as a colearners or coinvestigators than as instructors. Again, because we were new at problem-based learning and we did not have adequate bilingual resources, the activities were guided more by the teachers than we would have preferred. We now understand the significance of codevelopment with students.

Judging by the written and oral presentations, we believe that the children gained a lot of content and conceptual knowledge of their history, as well as improved literacy skills. According to our standards, many of them were very excited, curious, and motivated about their learning. A year later, they are still talking about the Aztecs and what they learned!

REFLECTING THE WORLD AROUND US: BUILDING MULTICULTURAL UNDERSTANDING

Claudette Rasmussen, Mary Brady, and William Munroe, *Marie Murphy School*

Overview of the Project

The overall goal of this seventh grade humanities unit was to investigate and build multicultural understanding. The unit was designed to use content from language arts skills and the social sciences and to strengthen problem solving skills by asking students to conduct research and engage in role-playing from the perspective of an ethnic group other than their own. The primary activity was that of a simulation of a newly configured high school where culturally diverse groups of students were electing their student government leaders. In the course of the simulation, students had to explore the opportunities and issues inherent in the problematic situation. These experiences caused them to consider the ways in which the simulated situation reflected real world problems and the ways in which they could build multicultural understanding in our diverse world.

This 12-week unit was codeveloped by social studies teacher, Mary Brady, language arts teacher, William Munroe, and me (one of the coauthors of the book). It was originally designed as an enrichment unit for a class of high-ability students. It was used in Marie Murphy's enrichment program for approximately 5 years before being integrated into Mary Brady's regular social studies classes. This unit serves as an example of how a challenging problem-oriented, student-centered curriculum—characteristics of many gifted programs—can meet the needs of a wide range of students within a heterogeneous classroom. Although this unit was designed and taught some years ago, its interdisciplinary, problem-based practices and its content are more timely than ever.

DESCRIPTION OF THE SCHOOL

Marie Murphy School is a junior high school in a school district of approximately 600 students, K-8, in an affluent suburb north of the city of Chicago. During the time that this unit was taught, it's student population was approximately 25% Asian and 75% Caucasian, including immigrants from Japan, Korea, eastern Europe, and Mediterranean countries. At the time that this unit was designed and taught, I was the coordinator of and a teacher in the Pupil Enrichment Program. My colleagues, Mary Brady and Bill Munroe, were long term teacher-leaders in the district. Mary had long-used simulation and role-playing in her social studies classrooms, Bill had always taught the full range of writing and speaking skills, and I had used numerous independent study projects with individuals and small groups of students over the years. However, this was the first time within our school that a team of teachers had collaborated on a problem-oriented interdisciplinary unit that incorporated all of these instructional strategies. We wrote the unit in about seven days one summer, team-taught it the following year, and then made refinements based on our instructional experiences. In the years that followed, it was taught by a single teacher, usually Mary or myself, within the enrichment program. Mary then incorporated it into her three regular social studies classes. She found that the open-ended nature of the task, together with well-structured student experiences, were highly succcessful with the full range of students within her classrooms. Of course, the need and desire for greater multicultural understanding applied to all.

RATIONALE FOR THE PROJECT

Purpose

This unit was intended to use language arts and social studies content to engage students in a long term, problem-based investigation of aspects of our multicultural society. The overall goal of the humanities unit was to develop multicultural literacy and a greater understanding of the complexities of the diverse society in which we live. Simulation, role-playing, and other instructional strategies used were designed to integrate multiple perspectives into a relatively homogeneous setting and to develop empathy for what it means to belong to various ethnic groups. It was hoped that this would be an effective means of building understanding of both self and others.

Research

"Reflecting the World Around Us: Building Multicultural Understanding" is an example of an integrative curriculum that incorporates aspects of both project-based and problem-based learning. Project-based learning, as described by Blumenfeld (1991), is characterized by projects that are relatively long-term, problem-focused, and a meaningful integration of concepts from a number of disciplines. This humanities unit incorporated the two essential components of projects:

❑ a problem that serves to structure and drive activities;

❑ activities that result in a series of artifacts or products that culminate in a final product that "answers" the driving question.

During the 10 to 12 week unit, students used research and role-playing to address the real-world problem of recognizing and appreciating cultural diversity. Each student kept a journal, often written from the perspective of another ethnic group, during a lengthy simulation of ethnic group interaction during a problematic situation. At the end of the simulation the journal mirrored each student's "identity's" actions and thoughts.

This real-life problem of building multicultural understanding had all the characteristics of the ill-structured problems described by Barrows (1988).

☐ The initial problem statement and problematic situation lacked all the essential information needed to understand the exact nature of the situation or problem and to decide what actions are required for resolution, if any.

☐ There was no absolutely right way to approach finding a resolution.

☐ As students gathered and shared information, the definition of the problem changed.

☐ Students could never be 100% sure they had made the "right" decisions because important information may have been lacking, and data or values may have been in conflict; still, decisions had to be made.

Although this humanities unit had many of the qualities of both problem-based and project-based learning, its designers were unaware of this theoretical base when they first developed, taught, and fine-tuned the curriculum. Instead they approached interdisciplinary curriculum design by: first identifying the characteristics and needs of their students; then by brainstorming possible attributes of conducive classroom climate, enriched content, enhanced thinking process, and challenging products; and finally by examining the most appropriate match of content and pedagogy to the developmental needs of the students. This integrative framework for curricular design (identified by the broad categories in view A) as well as some of the team's responses to those broad categories (listed in view B) are illustrated in Figure 9.

Our teacher team was certainly committed to the belief that schools have a responsibility to contribute to the development of multicultural literacy and understanding. The Curriculum Guidelines for Multicultural Education, adopted by the National Council for the Social Studies in 1976 and revised in 1991, provide a valuable research base for translating that belief into practice. Several of the 23 Guidelines have specific applications to this unit, namely that a multicultural curriculum should help students

☐ develop greater self-understanding.

☐ understand the many dimensions of ethnic experiences and cultures.

☐ understand that there will always be conflict between ideals and realities in human societies.

☐ develop values, attitudes, and behaviors that support cultural diversity while building a shared national culture.

☐ develop their decision-making and social participation skills and their sense of political efficacy.

☐ develop effective interpersonal, interethnic, and intercultural communications skills.

☐ interpret situations from diverse ethnic and cultural perspectives.

☐ make optimal use of experiential learning, particularly local community resources.

In fact, these guidelines recommended the role-playing of various ethnic and cultural experiences as one means of building greater understanding of what it means to belong to various ethnic groups.

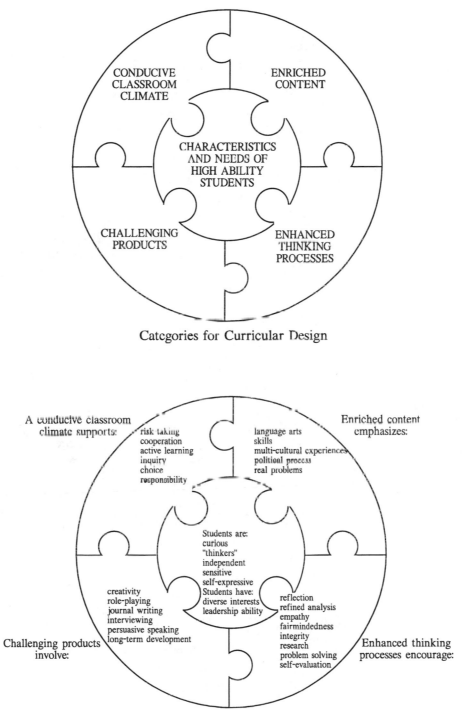

Categories for Curricular Design

Attributes/Elements of Curriculum

Figure 9 *Integrative framework for curricular design. Copyright 1988, Avoca School District #37. Used by permission.*

Broad Student Outcomes

When planning our multicultural unit, we identified the *enrichment objectives* for all interdisciplinary activities and the ways in which these objectives would replace and extend learning of the *core objectives* of the regular Language Arts Skills class during which this course was taught. These local student outcomes were described in an excerpt from our own curriculum guide.

> CORE OBJECTIVES: Using oral language to persuade; developing ideas with appropriate support; presenting ideas with appropriate introduction, elaboration and conclusion; and using appropriate and varied reference materials to research a topic using the library, the mass media, people, and personal observation.

> ENRICHMENT OBJECTIVES: Role playing using intellectual empathy, fair-mindedness, integrity, and perseverance; understanding the need for compromise; speaking extemporaneously; using higher levels of persuasion; incorporating and creating projects to enhance presentations; understanding the political process by participating in a simulated campaign; recognizing a wide range of political beliefs and how they are integrated into a party platform; understanding similarities and differences within and among six ethnic groups; appreciating the opportunities and challenges of a multicultural society; using questions that probe reasons and evidence, differing viewpoints, implications and consequences. (*Pupil Enrichment Program Curriculum Guide,* Brady, Munroe, & Rasmussen, 1987, p. 1)

Broad Task and Ill-Structured Problem or Questions

The broad task was to engage students in research and role-playing in order to build multicultural understanding. By taking on an ethnic identity other than their own and participating in the simulation of a problematic situation, students encountered numerous subproblems and issues and had to find ways to respond to them.

FLOW OF THE PROJECT AND SAMPLE ACTIVITIES AND ASSESSMENTS

The introduction to this course began with a discussion of the unit title, "Reflecting the World Around Us: Building Multicultural Understanding." Students shared their interpretations of its meaning, particularly in relationship to the multicultural society we live in, and we described possible problems, issues, and opportunities that it might raise.

Students were then involved in a brief introductory commercial simulation, "Rafa Rafa," so that they might discover some of the differences in beliefs and behaviors of Alphans and Betans, members of two different "societies." Following a debriefing of learnings from the experience, we codeveloped behavioral guidelines for role-playing to support multicultural understanding. Guidelines incorporated those behaviors specific to multicultural simulations (e.g., "keeping in character," "taking seriously the beliefs and behaviors of another culture even when they're different," "showing respect for other cultures' beliefs by being ready to learn why they believe what they believe"). Guidelines also addressed behaviors important for any cooperative learning experience, including "accepting other's ideas and showing openmindedness," "trying to understand other people's ways and showing empathy," and "looking at all points of view before making a judgment, and showing fair-mindedness."

We then began the lengthy SPECTRUM II simulation, a greatly expanded and revised version of a simulation originally written by Andrea Taylor in 1975. As a design team of teachers, we had: added many activities to structure this high school simulation for our 7th grade students; revised it to reflect the current demographics of the city of Chicago and our suburb; embedded historical and current research activities in it; and placed it in the context of a larger humanities unit with a guiding problem-based theme.

Phase I of the Spectrum II simulation provided an introduction to the problem situation and facilitated students' role identification. Students and teachers discussed the situation described below.

SPECTRUM II: A Simulation

PURPOSE: Shifting ethnic populations are having significant impact across the United States as students of different ethnic backgrounds are coming together in various schools and neighborhoods. Formerly predominantly White schools have become a "spectrum" of assorted cultural groups. The purpose of this simulation is to give you a chance to assume roles involving many of the different ethnic groups present in society today. While assuming these roles, you can gain new insights into situations involving conflict, consensus, and interpersonal relationships. A second function of the simulation is to provide you with a setting where you can discover the wide variety of factors that can affect the outcome of an election, factors such as personalities, prejudices, special interests, quest for personal gain, and current issues and problems.

BACKGROUND

CITY: Stoney Point is a suburb of a large metropolitan area. Living in homes whose prices are all over $150,000, its residents are primarily well-to-do business persons and professionals with family incomes over $70,000 per year. Most residents are White, although an increasing number of Asians also live in the suburb. The neighboring metropolitan area has a diverse population made up of several ethnic groups who live in largely separate neighborhoods.

ATTENDANCE BOUNDARIES: Recently, the lines of Stoney Point High's school district were redrawn. Several neighborhoods within the fringe of the nearby city limits were given the opportunity to send their youth to Stoney Point High School. Sons and daughters of White, Black, Hispanic, and Native American blue collar workers suddenly found themselves mingling with upper middle-class and upper class Stoney Point youth.

SITUATION: The ethnic groups living in the fringe of the city have always remained relatively isolated from each other. In the past minor incidents have resulted from occasional friction among groups. Now, after a summer of redistricting, all six groups have been thrown together at Stoney Point High School.

ELECTION COMING: School has been open for several weeks. It is now time for the election of this year's student government leaders. Two political parties have emerged, the Moderates and the Radicals. Each party is developing a platform to explain its candidates' views on the major issues and problems affecting Stoney Point High School students. (*Pupil Enrichment Program Curriculum Guide,* Brady et al., 1987, p.11)

Following a discussion for understanding, students drew for roles of an ethnic group other than their own. Then each student began a journal with the first entry focusing on answers to questions that they asked of themselves in their new roles (i.e., "Why do you think that your parent(s) decided to send you or continue to send you to

Stoney Point High?" "How do you feel about that?" "Consider what it's been like for you to be at Stoney Point for a few weeks now. Describe some of your experiences. . . .", "What do you think might happen during the upcoming student elections?")

Following this opportunity to react and predict, students stepped out-of-role to work in small ethnic-alike groups to conduct research on their new-found ethnic identities. Using "The American Story" tape series from B'nai B'rith, they explored three generations of an American family, i.e., the Hernandez family or the Fukiyama family, and read and discussed accompanying historical writings. They conducted research on current events and issues and interviewed representatives from the Chicago-based Midwest Bilingual Education Multifunctional Resource Center. After each type of research, students considered the implications for their roles.

In a "Create-a-Character" activity, students used the research and their imaginations to develop characterization by responding to questions about their characters' physical description, interests, personality, habits, fears, values, strengths, weaknesses, family, friends, and motivation.

Students then worked individually and with group members to complete the "Putting Yourself in the Other Person's Place" activity that follows.

Putting Yourself in the Other Person's Place

Soon you will be climbing the stairs of Stoney Point High. In order to help you step into your role, it will be important for you to empathize with your character by "putting yourself in the other person's place."

The following questions will help you to take what you've learned about the past and present and further apply that to your character's daily behavior—his or her values, beliefs, attitudes, feelings, thoughts, actions.

Take 15–20 minutes to answer the following questions individually. Then discuss them with other members of your ethnic group. Add any ideas from the group to your individual descriptors.

In what ways would the experience of entering Stoney Point be similar or different from desegregation experiences of 15–20 years ago?

How is your ethnic group typically portrayed in the media? How would your portrayal be different than the stereotypes of your ethnic group on television or in other media?

Who will be your character's "role models"?

How strongly will your ethnic group, in general, and your character, in particular, feel about maintaining ethnic identity? How will your character demonstrate ethnic ties on a day-to-day basis (music, clothes, food, religion, etc.)?

Activities in Phase I of SPECTRUM II demonstrate how teachers can carefully structure activities around a non-trivial problem, yet facilitate the students' own development of increasingly refined responses to aspects of the problem. The journal introduced in Phase I was kept throughout the simulation and evaluated periodically by the teachers.

The ethnic identity journal as well as other products developed during "the political process" of Phases II–IV became the artifacts of students' increasing multicultural understanding and frequent applications of specific language arts and social studies skills. The following excerpt (intended for students) from the curriculum guide illustrates, once again, how such discovery activities can be carefully structured around an otherwise ill-structured problem.

The Political Process

CAMPAIGNING: Campaigning will take place throughout three events—a Party Forum, a Press Conference, and a Political Rally. These events will give members of both the Moderate and Radical tickets opportunities to use persuasive tactics to swing the Independent votes to their party. Since Independent voters are the key to the election, students who are Independent can exert considerable influence on candidates through questioning and other "lobbying" efforts.

Placards on behalf of individual candidates or political parties can be displayed in the classroom by that candidate or party at any time during the campaign.

PARTY FORUM:

- Independents identify 5 issues from the "Student Problems and Issues" sheet. Issues are put on board for use by candidates.

- Independents prepare questions about the issues they identified as most important. The same questions will be asked of candidates from both parties.

- Each candidate makes a brief opening statement about their stand on the identified issues.

- The teacher, acting as Moderator, asks the designated candidate from each party to respond to a specific question on the identified issue, continuing until all questions have been asked.

- Each candidate makes a brief closing statement that includes his or her reactions to other candidates' responses to questions and a restatement of his or her own stand on the issues.

PRESS CONFERENCE:

☐ Independents can ask any question of any candidate on any issue, campaign statement, or event.

☐ Each candidate should be prepared to answer any question.

☐ The teacher, acting as "press secretary," will moderate the conference.

POLITICAL RALLY:

☐ Each candidate will give a job-specific and platform-oriented persuasive speech during this final campaign event.

☐ Each Independent will give a speech on behalf of a party, individual candidate, or on behalf of an Independent stand (if no candidate or party has, as yet, satisfied him or her on the issues).

☐ Party members may bring leaflets, posters, buttons, banners, etc., and sign any songs or jingles they have written.

☐ Following the Rally, "lobbying" can continue up until the time of the election.

> ELECTION: You will be asked to vote twice—once as you think your character would vote and once as you, your real self, would vote. (*Pupil Enrichment Program Curriculum Guide,* Brady et al., 1987, pp. 26–27)

As you can imagine, varied and alternative forms of assessment had to be used throughout the simulation. The journal was evaluated periodically on the basis of the thoughtfulness, thoroughness, and role-appropriateness of the entries. The persuasive speeches, given during the Political Rally, were evaluated on the basis of presentation skills, persuasiveness, use of campaign materials and the party platform, presentation of issues and proposals, and support of proposals. Significant student and teacher evaluation took place in the final debriefing phase of the simulation. Students reflected on the various factors that influenced their voting decisions and role-playing by using a questionnaire (excerpts follow).

Debriefing Questions

Our simulation of ethnic group interaction during a student government election is over. We ask you to take your last step out of the door of Stoney Point High and to reenter the familiar surroundings of Marie Murphy Junior High. However, before "life returns to normal" in the halls and classrooms, we ask you to think carefully about the following questions.

First answer these questions by yourself, after reviewing your journal. Tomorrow you will have the opportunity to discuss your answers within a small "cross-cultural" group. Following that discussion, you will be able to add to or change your opinions and ideas and write your responses below.

1. Did you feel the roles were realistic? Why or why not?

2. Did your feelings towards your role I.D. change as the simulation progressed? If so, how and why? If not, why not?

4. How did different campaign tactics affect you?

6. Compare the way you voted in your role with the way you voted as yourself. What do you conclude?

10. What insights into some problems caused by tensions among students and ethnic groups did the simulation give you?

11. How would you change the simulation to improve it or make it more realistic?

12. What did you like about the simulation?

Teachers assessed these responses using the same criteria as they did for the journal entries. Finally, students responded to the essay questions below intended to measure growth in multicultural understanding during the semester-long class. Students and teachers evaluated answers to these questions. Following that, the questions were used in whole group debriefing.

Essay Questions

> Give careful thought to these questions before writing your answers in informal essay form. Your answers will be graded on the basis of your thoroughness and thoughtfulness as you reflect on the semester's experiences—the "Rafa Rafa," simulation, historical study of an ethnic group, the SPECTRUM II simulation, and study of current information and issues about race relations in Chicago and the United States.

1. List some of the similarities between the "Rafa Rafa" and SPECTRUM II simulations and real life. (Consider actions, beliefs, issues, feelings, etc.)

3. What thoughts, feelings, problems, and insights would you experience if your family were to move to another part of the Chicago metropolitan area or the United States where the ethnic groups were different from your previous neighborhood?

4. What qualities, attitudes and/or skills are important for a person who is "role-playing" cross-cultural situations and who is actually living, working or playing in a community that is economically and ethnically mixed?

5. In what ways do you feel you have accomplished the purposes of our class?

REFLECTION AND SELF-ASSESSMENT

I hope that the examples from this humanities unit illustrate not only the complexity of integrative instruction but also the richness and power of such interdisciplinary, problem-based instruction.

Throughout the unit nearly all of the indicators of engaged learning were applied to some extent. Clearly, students had a high degree of responsibility for their own learning in individual role-playing and journaling, small group research and campaign preparation, and whole group discussion. In fact, students were almost always in the roles of explorer and producer. Teachers most often stepped back, acting as facilitators and guides primarily through the careful design of instructional activities and materials, monitoring and questioning during actual instruction only when needed. Grouping was flexible. Sometimes students were placed in cross-cultural groups to encourage multiple perspectives. Sometimes they were placed in ethnic-alike groups for common knowledge building. Students were also highly collaborative, developing many new understandings through their role-playing, research, and debriefing with each other.

This unit with its long-term rather intense approach to the complex task of building multicultural understanding was a very challenging one for the students. At times it was difficult for them to stay in role, to be true to their character. At times they were frustrated by the lack of any clear-cut resolution to the very human problems and issues they were encountering. It became increasingly important to provide opportunities for them to step out of role so that they could reflect, debrief their learnings along the way, and lend support to one another. Stepping in and out of role, journaling, and debriefing engaged students in a progressive problem-solving process.

Students certainly did feel as if they were all in this together! The requirement of taking on an ethnic identity other than one's own was a great leveler—everyone was equal in that sense. The role-playing, together with the research, also created a great deal of empathy for the experiences of other cultural groups.

Although we relied heavily on simulation, in many ways the tasks were authentic. The conditions of the simulation reflected the demographics of the greater metropolitan area in which students lived. Care was taken to include quality historical and contemporary research, and there was an opportunity to interview representatives of cultural groups in the area. Still, I think that there would be greater authenticity with less simulation and more contact with the diverse real world around us. A field trip to ethnic neighborhoods in Chicago and on-line communications with members of other cultural groups or other students and adults with a similar purpose would add a great deal to this unit. It would also temper some of the frustrations students felt, and help them to sustain a high degree of interest throughout this long unit.

Another way in which I would modify the planning for this unit would be to incorporate more aspects of codevelopment with students. The design approach that our teacher team used was a parallel one to early steps in the preliminary planning process of the PBL-CD model presented in Goal 3 of this book. We did an effective job of considering and integrating the needs of students with our curricular content, thinking process, and assessment needs. We could have shifted more from a thematic, project-based study to the problem-based study represented in the PBL-CD model by making the broad problem more explicit in question form and by involving students in identifying subproblems and subquestions and structuring their investigations around them. Their investigations would be especially strong if they resulted in recommendations for ways in which to strengthen multicultural understanding in our school community.

Finally, I would enhance this unit by further integrating some of the guidelines for multicultural education from the National Council for the Social Studies (1991; described in the Research section) into the instructional activities.

Still, this humanities unit as taught was a powerful one for a wide range of students over several years. With each class, it definitely accomplished its goal of building multicultural understanding as well as a greater understanding of self, others, and the world around us.

SELF-DIRECTED ACTIVITIES

In this activity, we will focus on *Phase 3: Conducting Inquiry & Analysis.*

1a **Understanding the Teacher-Authors' PBL-CD Units:** Compare and contrast ideas from the two PBL-CD units. What useful ideas have these teacher authors incorporated into their PBL-CD units? Which ideas are unique to each unit and which are common to both units? Record them in the appropriate areas of this Venn diagram:

Building on Children's Capital
by Exploring Our Aztec Past

Reflecting the World Around Us:
Building Multicultural Understanding

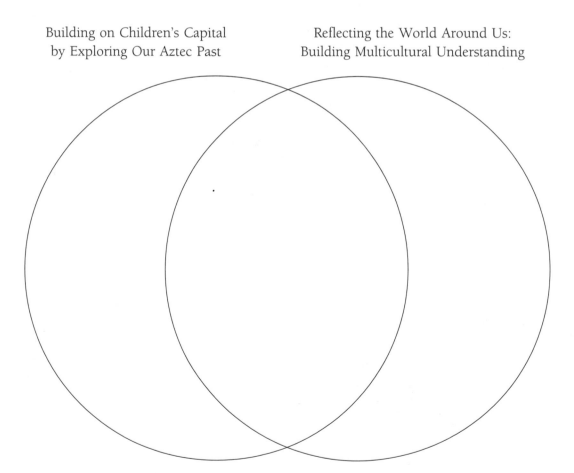

1b **Understanding and Planning for Your PBL-CD Units:** *Phase 3—Conducting Inquiry and Analysis.* Using Goal 3 and Appendix C as references, what ideas from the Venn would be most useful to you as you build upon plans in preparation for Phase 3?

Think about how these ideas and ideas from earlier units will help you to prepare for Phase 3 of progressive problem solving in the classroom: What teaching and learning strategies will help you and your students identify specific problems? What teacher roles and student roles will be most appropriate throughout this phase?

Teacher Roles	Teaching Goals and Strategies	Student Roles	Learning Strategies and Responsibilities

2 **Acting and Sharing:** When you have completed a draft of possible instructional activities for Phase 3, share your ideas with a critical friend team. Describe your plans for your informal conference below.
Process for a critical friend dialogue:

❏ share your desired outcome for the conversation
❏ ask your critical friend to practice active listening and ask clarifying questions
❏ offer constructive, nonjudgmental feedback

3 **Reflecting:** Reflect upon the outcomes of your critical friend conference. List or in some way represent them (metaphor, graphic organizer, icon).

4 **Rethinking and Refining:** What are the implications for you/your team's unit plan?

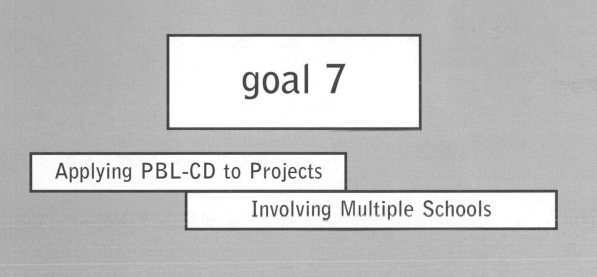

goal 7

Applying PBL-CD to Projects

Involving Multiple Schools

The two Profiles in this Goal are parallel to the PLB-CD model in two ways. First, both projects provide problem-based learning opportunities to multiple schools, though the models are quite different from each other and from the PBL-CD model used in previous Goals. Second, both projects involve some level of codevelopment with teachers.

"Discovery Channel Learning Community: *The Promised Land* Project," developed by Duggan and Duggan, is about how to create a telecommunity on the Internet as a model for involving teachers in problem- and project-based learning. Their Profile focuses broadly on problems and issues related to the migration of African Americans from Mississippi to Chicago in the 1930s, as portrayed in the Discovery Channel's documentary, *The Promised Land*.

The Promised Land Project is presented on the World Wide Web (www) and so is open for anyone to participate in. The teaching units that result from use of this Web site are an interaction of the goals and characteristics of those who come to the site and of those who manage the site. This means that in many regards what a student or school gets out of the site depends heavily on what is put into it. Most www sites feature only descriptive text or interactive information resources. The Duggans have created a www site that provides rich information and human resources to schools, forming the basis for a community in which all users may interact and contribute. In essence, this project and a few others like it are redefining learning at a distance by moving the focus from transmitting information toward more interactive, project-based, and problem-based learning.

In "Problems as Possibilities: Transforming Garbage into Gold," Finkle and Torp from the Illinois Mathematics and Science Academy (IMSA), codeveloped problem-based learning units with teacher teams from nine schools. The schools were all quite different from each other, some being urban, some suburban, some high school, and some elementary. In this project, the authors developed a model curriculum unit on issues related to dealing with garbage that teachers could use, as is, as a simulation; or use as the basis for a variation using local issues and resources. In either case, the author team and their colleagues structure and closely monitor the process for PBL. They draw upon a research base that combines the medical model of PBL promoted by imsa for schools, but also add a strong element of PBL as service learning. That is, the problem to be solved is a community problem. Additionally, this Profile illustrates the increasingly important role that schools are playing as leaders in curricular reform.

DISCOVERY CHANNEL LEARNING COMMUNITY: *THE PROMISED LAND* PROJECT

Will Duggan and Andree Duggan, *Discovery Educational Relations, Interactive FrameWorks, Inc.*

Overview of the Project

During 1995, the Discovery Channel had its premier showing of a series called *The Promised Land*, which was based on the novel by Nicholas Lemann. This series documented the migration of African Americans from Mississippi to Chicago in the 1930s and 1940s. Educators could tape the commercial-free version for use in schools. Discovery Communications, Inc., convened a design team to develop a virtual learning environment to sustain interest and inquiry about this historical event; this virtual learning environment became known as *The Promised Land* Learning Community. The design team identified resources, relationships, and collaborative activities that were easily accessed by World Wide Web (www), Gopher, file transfer protocol (ftp), and e-mail. What we report here is the pilot project that ran from Fall of 1994 to Fall of 1995.[1]

The overarching goal of the project was to encourage participants to produce original, authentic scholarship and artistic expression about this century's "Promised Land" migrations and to explore the implications of these movements for contemporary America. Toward that end, the www site is rich with discussion groups, student-produced materials, exchanges of information and data, and communications among students, artists, craft specialists, musicians, researchers, and persons who have experienced group migration. The project's timely theme and resources provide many opportunities for problem- and project-based learning.

---

[1]The project was developed for Discovery Communications, Inc. It is the codesign of Hunter Williams, Senior Manager, Discovery, and Andree and Will Duggan of Interactive FrameWorks, Inc., a Maryland-based telecommunications consulting firm. Gopher and Web design consultation and implementation is being provided by the AskEric project at the Eric Clearinghouse on Information & Technology, Syracuse University, and the InfoMail program of the Northeast Parallel Architecture Center, also located at Syracuse University.

The project is primarily geared for use with junior high and high school students, although elementary school students and teachers have found appropriate activities in relationship to the project. Undergraduate and graduate students, doctoral candidates, and a wide range of experts from institutions of higher learning, research, and cultural centers are serving as local coaches and "telementors," listserv[2] moderators, and occasional contributors. Additionally, thousands of interested persons of all ages are visiting the Internet and America On-line sites to engage in listserv discussions and private correspondence with teachers and students.

RATIONALE FOR THE PROJECT

Purpose

The *Promised Land* Learning Community was developed to help students and others use Discovery Channel programming in innovative ways that promote engaged learning and integration of emerging telecommunications technologies. More specifically, the design team wanted to use various interdisciplinary themes related to migration, African American history, race relations, language arts, economics, and artistic and cultural expression to support a wide diversity of connections to the subject areas (i.e., history, contemporary issues, geography, social studies, and even biology and chemistry). The goal was to create a synergy between the Internet maxim of "users as producers" and the problem-based learning principle of students as cocreators of new knowledge. The most critical task was to develop strategies for teachers and students to feel ownership over the project as a whole and their contributions to it.

Research

Much has been written about the information revolution and the changing roles of information producers and providers (e.g., Information Task Force, Committee on

---

[2]Listservs describe the software that provides opportunities for people with similar interests to communicate using e-mail. Listservs allow one subscriber to communicate with many other subscribers by sending messages through one address.

Applications and Technology, 1994). Traditionally, most schools depend very heavily on textbooks that supply most, if not all, of the necessary instruction, assessments, and ancillary materials. Thus, these providers support a transmission model of learning in which learners acquire the information that is provided. Jones, Valdez, Nowakowski, and Rasmussen (1995) argue that schools and other educational institutions will turn increasingly to what they call the "New Providers" of content for students and of professional development.

Some New Providers offer global information content and resources, such as weather data from nasa's earth stations, or support virtual learning communities using public information resources such as zoos, libraries, and museums. (See References for the addresses of two New Providers: Academy One and the World Wide Web for the Coalition of Essential Schools.) Others provide valuable information services such as designing software that helps students visualize and understand what they see. What these groups have in common is that they support active learning and interdisciplinary projects around authentic tasks, and they often provide links between students and experts and role models.

Although the concepts for the *Promised Land* Learning Community have been evolving for several years, the New Providers concept helped us focus on design questions. How can we develop a virtual learning community around a powerful documentary television series so that learners are engaged in authentic tasks that are meaningful and challenging? How can we design telecommunications tools that help students and others interact with data and resources in user-friendly ways? How do we create conditions for knowledge building among wide ranging age groups and interests? We believe that the pilot we have designed could be a model for others to use the Internet and other telecommunications to change fundamentally the nature of learning at a distance, working toward building a telecommunity in which user interest and contributions become self-sustaining.

Other sources of research that have helped shape the *Promised Land* Learning Community include the APA Presidential Task Force (1993), which developed the learner-centered psychology principles referred to in various places in this book; and Checkoway and Flynn (1993), who discussed new roles for students as producers and community builders. These seminal works envision new student and teacher roles in very social, low-risk environments that are highly supportive of critical thinking, problem solving, and independent learning. In addition, these works (among others; e.g., Jones et al., 1995) emphasize the importance of authentic tasks.[3]

Components of the Project

On the basis of the research and much thought, we developed the Web site for the *Promised Land* Learning Community using a variety of components. Figure 10 illustrates the major components of the site and how they fit together. The major components may be defined as follows:

1. *Unifying Theme.* The unifying theme of migration will support (a) diverse subthemes and (b) various subject areas. Examples of project subthemes include exploring family histories; determining the chemistry and nutrition of favorite family reunion foods; using technology to map the patterns of migration; exploring similar migration experiences; comparing and contrasting how blues and spirituals have evolved; using oral histories in English-as-a-Second-Language classes; and linking themes in the Promised Land to other works of literature and to U.S. history. Subject areas for the Project include history, social studies, the performing arts, the humanities, chemistry, nutrition, political science, and economics.

2. *Facilitators.* Our job is to create the community: identify people who enrich the Learning Community; conceptualize potential connections to education; moderate online discussions; help make matches of classroom activities with learning resources, relationships, and related activities; coordinate the student-mentor and student-teacher

---

[3]The Promised Land Learning Community can be found at the following address: http:\\www.discovery.com/school.

FACILITATORS

AUTHENTIC
SCHOLARSHIP for
AUTHENTIC
AUDIENCES

COMMUNITY
CONNECTIONS

UNIFYING
THEME

COMMUNICATION
CHANNELS and
SUPPORT STRUCTURES

COLLABORATIVE
ACTIVITIES

Figure 10 *Learning community components. Copyright 1995, Interactive Frameworks, Inc. Used by permission.*

contribution process; edit and help publish contributions from participants; evolve and refresh the Learning Community over time. Facilitators as well as community members help teachers see how to use resources creatively. For example, an English teacher might want help in utilizing some of the resources for art and music. We might also help teachers see the same theme from multiple perspectives or link them to sound research and practice.

3. *Community Connections.* These are the people, resources, and organizations, such as museums, that the facilitators bring on board to work either locally or virtually with classrooms to enrich the learning experience. Prescreened telementors are accomplished artists, business people, community leaders, and scholars who are ready, willing, and able to work with students and teachers locally or in cyberspace.

4. *Collaborative Activities.* Some projects initiated by the facilitators are open-ended invitations to contribute small pieces to a "virtual quilt." For example, making an African American timeline becomes one square in a broad effort to

gather historical data. In other instances, teachers and students create projects to advance specific educational objectives. In all instances, communications are diverse: students teachers, experts, community members, and others communicate with each other throughout the project.

5. *Communication Channels and Support Structures.* Our list-serv discussion allows community members to use e-mail to post interests, queries, references, and opinions. This discussion serves as a self-perpetuating match-maker that brings together people who share common interests in the theme of migration and subthemes such as race relations or evolution of the blues. The on-line discussion may also bring together those interested in pedagogy such as the development of interdisciplinary projects, the use of telecommunication technologies, and community-based learning. Additionally, participants can access

◻ information about the documentary series.

◻ frameworks and approaches for academic achievement.

◻ accruing references (e.g., books, films, exhibitions) and Internet resources.

◻ special projects such as a discussion on leadership in which African Americans of all ages participate, sponsored by Academy One.

6. *Authentic Scholarship for Authentic Audiences.* The entire project can be seen as an effort to support the production of original scholarship and insight from students, working alone or in teams, or as cocreators with practicing professionals. The www site of the Learning Community houses the Student Showcase with a full array of original student reports, artwork, oral history transcripts, musical compositions and other products from locally innovated projects, as well as results from on-line networking projects. The long-term goal of the facilitators is to index the Showcase so that this work can become more useful to others with an interest in a particular area, such as Chicago in the '30s or Mexican immigration.

Student contributions to the Learning Community are published through a three-stage communication process with the project designers: a one-sentence "idea"; a one-page "plan"; and the final presentation. This process provides an opportunity for the Learning Community design team and facilitators to suggest resources, relationships, and activities and to network like-minded efforts. Participants are also encouraged to provide updates throughout the process as well as post interesting findings and queries to the listserv discussions.

FLOW OF PROJECT

The Promised Land Learning Community has entered its second year in 1996. What follows is a brief summary of what took place from September 1994 throughout 1995. Figure 11 shows the development of the project.

First, we determined that the project focus would be *The Promised Land*—a compelling saga, somewhat unsung, that would help distinguish our work as a telecommunity investigating interdisciplinary themes from what we saw as a plethora of on-line efforts in mathematics and science. Then we conducted a field survey of "things connected with *The Promised Land*" and developed a project description, which served as a basis for conversations with people who might bring resources to the Learning Community. We conducted "win-win" dialogues to negotiate what each person or group would bring to the community and what they would take from it. At this point, we were ready to involve pilot schools that we knew were interested in project- or problem-based learning or integration of Internet technologies with learning. We heard about the potential classrooms through the on-line grapevine (e.g., discussions at the Consortium for School Networking, Internet surveys, chance meetings, recommendations of knowledgeable persons).

We spent many hours linking teachers and other school staff to our telementors and other resources at the site. We actively used the garden metaphor in our work: planting. It seemed to us that we were bringing together the elements to help things grow—nutrients, water, sunlight.

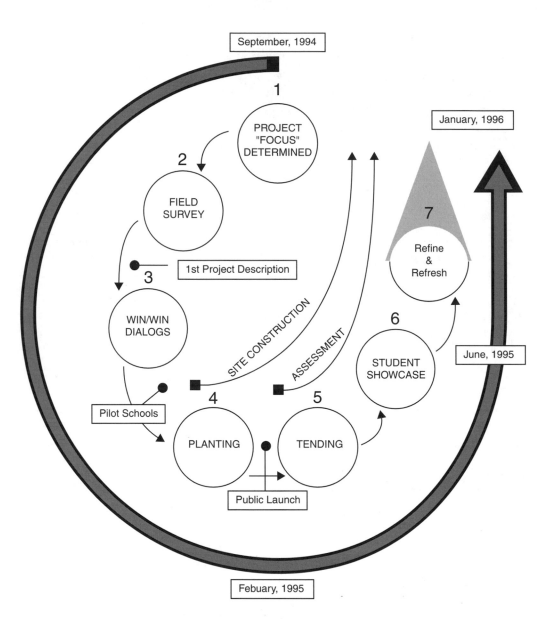

September, 1994

1
PROJECT "FOCUS" DETERMINED

2
FIELD SURVEY

January, 1996

1st Project Description

3
WIN/WIN DIALOGS

7
Refine & Refresh

SITE CONSTRUCTION

ASSESSMENT

Pilot Schools

6
STUDENT SHOWCASE

June, 1995

4
PLANTING

5
TENDING

Public Launch

Febuary, 1995

Figure 11 *Flowchart for* The Promised Land *learning community. Copyright 1995, Interactive Frameworks, Inc. Used by permission.*

When we saw seedlings growing, we were ready for a Public Launching (announcement) of the project. Tending our "garden" involved proactive production, matchmaking, and handholding. Proactive work involved such things as commissioning a guide to oral histories or facilitating activities with Academy One. Handholding meant doing whatever was necessary to get people feeling comfortable enough to do what they had said they would do (e.g., "Do you have your e-mail address yet?" or refining the www and gopher sites).

SAMPLE PROJECTS AND ACTIVITIES

New Places Project

One of the most popular projects for elementary schools has been the New Places Project, a collaboration between the *Promised Land* Learning Community and I*EARN, an international initiative supported by the Copen Foundation. This project was designed to be a mechanism for social and ethnic groups within schools to talk to each other and to facilitate the adjustments of students recently arrived at the school. The idea is that these new students become local experts because in order to participate in the project other students need to talk to them about their experiences in other countries or places. The challenge to students is to express personal feelings about the moving or migration experience, and to work collaboratively with other students and faculty to make school a better place for newcomers. Exhibit 4 is an essay produced by a fourth grader from San Francisco who had recently arrived from Mexico. The essay was presented along with a photo of the sewing. Other

| Exhibit 4 | My Sewing |

The sewing is a symbol of Mexico. The mountains remind me of Mexico. It has a cactus, a house, cloud, and sky. People are immigrating from Mexico to the United States.

I chose these things because it is important for me not to forget where my parents are from and to be happy to be a Mexican American. I want people to know that all our family is proud. I also want people to know that they should not be ashamed of themselves. So my scene represents my love for my family and our culture.

It is important to me that we don't laugh at their color. I think it must be hard when people get caught when they are coming to the United States.

Johnny Tegeda, Paul Revere Primary, 4th Grade, San Francisco.

ways to participate in the project include Internet discussions across schools and countries.

Mentoring Activities

A major appeal of telecommunications technology is the capacity to provide schools with human resources that would otherwise not be available. The Learning Community has provided many prescreened mentors who apparently had at least as much reward from their experiences as the students. For example, John Beckley is an artist who uses iron casting to make sculptures. As part of his mentorship, he used both telecommunications and local visits to teach some students about his technique. Later he invited them to join him in a workshop he was giving. John Beckley told us that

> . . . In May of 1995, Suitland students, Michael Young, Adrian Britt, and I conducted a mini-workshop about their casting experience. This was quite exciting for the students, and for me as well. The workshop took place during a showing of my work which was part of a national tour of African American Craft Art. I went that day thinking I would probably be the main presenter, but within a few minutes, I was pleased to see the boys taking the lead with the audience and begin teaching everything they had learned themselves. The whole experience was personally gratifying. (personal communication, May 1995)

REFLECTION AND SELF-ASSESSMENT

We view the pilot as an important first step to provide a design that advances the dynamics of authentic tasks, improved access to data and resources, knowledge-building in the context of a Learning Community, and interaction with practicing professionals and community members. That said, there is a long way to go, especially in terms of the economic and administrative support of cultural changes (classrooms without walls) and connectivity (both real and virtual) so that teachers, learners, and mentors can take on and innovate new roles and responsibilities.

The facilitators can attest to the amount of interpersonal support, training, and support services that are required to help teachers, learners, and mentors explore new roles, interrelationships, and learning activities. Teachers, learners, and mentors needed help getting on-line, gaining the confidence to shape their own innovations, and shifting from a passive dependence on having materials provided to proactively seeking out new materials and relationships and incorporating that search into the authentic learning process.

With hindsight, we were clearly expecting too much to have students share presentations and materials produced for others so quickly. Perhaps the central issue we had to address was the ease with which teachers and learners make connections between *Promised Land* activities and prescribed learning outcomes. A few classrooms did an excellent job of connecting activities to curriculum objectives. Many more contributions, however, were exciting and involved learning but were not well-integrated into the curriculum. Also contributions were delayed by tests, graduations, summer vacations, and other events. In our minds, the delay showcasing student scholarship has been instructive. In future efforts, we have to do a better job of helping teachers and learners understand how participation in the Learning Community and production of authentic scholarship can make a better match with academic achievement and curriculum goals. We believe adequate lead time is key.

We feel that participation in the *Promised Land* Learning Community would be more fluent if the community members had had the indicators of engaged learning provided by Jones et. al. (1995) as a common vocabulary to have a better understanding about the dynamics of good learning experiences. This project was a pilot, and pilots are intended for design teams and facilitators to learn from their mistakes. We are refining and refreshing the Learning Community for release in 1996, incorporating and organizing the vast community contributions and resource ideas.

Sheryl L. Finkle and Linda T. Torp, *Illinois Mathematics and Science Academy*

Overview of the Project

In the summer of 1994, the Illinois Mathematics and Science Academy's (IMSA) Center for Problem-Based Learning[4] and the Illinois State Board of Education (ISBE) began a 3-year, multiphase collaboration to engage students statewide in authentic service learning experiences that were problem based. The planning team for this project wanted to provide students with educational opportunities to engage in community problem-solving while enriching academic learning, promoting ethical decision-making, and developing skills necessary for productive citizenship.

During the first phase of the collaboration, IMSA staff worked with ISBE staff to design and implement the project. Our task as professional developers was to provide selected teachers in Illinois with the appropriate background knowledge and skills, materials, and mentorship to codevelop and implement with their students an interdisciplinary problem-based learning unit centered on an authentic ill-structured problem related to a common issue. The issue of garbage and managing waste was chosen because of its universal nature and the ability of teachers and students from a wide variety of urban, suburban, and rural settings to connect with this relevant situation.

During the fall of 1994, we worked with approximately 50 teachers from nine schools (K–12) in a series of six full-

[4]The Illinois Mathematics and Science Academy's Center for Problem-Based Learning has been funded through the Harris Family Foundation.

The model landfill problem used in this project was first developed for the IMSA Summer Challenge Program which was funded by the Alfred P. Sloan Foundation, the Lloyd A. Fry Foundation, the Amoco Foundation, Ameritech Illinois, and the Illinois Power Company.

The efforts of the participating school teams in the development and implementation of their problem-based learning and service learning units were supported in part through funds from the Learn and Serve America Program administered by the Illinois State Board of Education.

day design and implementation sessions. We assisted each school team in finding an appropriate garbage-related problem within their own community and creating a problem-based curriculum focused on this situation. Using a prototype landfill problem as a model, teachers designed units and prepared accompanying teaching and learning plans taking into account the school's culture, the students' learning needs and abilities, and district outcomes (Finkle, et al., 1994).

Whereas four of the nine teacher teams chose to use the landfill simulation, the remaining units that emerged placed students in the midst of wide-ranging, authentic, problematic situations. These included reducing waste at school by community recycling; moving large-scale incineration in the neighborhood to the location of county landfills; and the safe and legal disposal of biohazardous waste dating from 1939 located in the basement of a hospital. The problem takes anywhere from one to three weeks to come to resolution depending on time allotted in the daily schedule, the range of issues and subissues students explore, and the medium of exploration (i.e., field trips, experimentation, reading, community contact).

DESCRIPTION OF THE SCHOOLS

IMSA was established through state legislation with a two-part mission. One aspect of this mission is to serve the needs of over 600 students talented in mathematics and science. We maintain the nation's only 3-year public residential high school. The other aspect of our mission is to serve the needs of the school districts in the state in transforming mathematics and science teaching and learning. For this reason the Academy supports an extensive program of professional development through institutes, partnerships, and sustained relationships with school-based teams. To provide substantive support for one such professional development focus, IMSA established the Center for Problem-Based Learning. The Center promotes, researches, and facilitates educators' inquiry into problem-based learning for K-12 schools.

Project staff included Dr. Sheryl Finkle, Coordinator for Teacher Development in the Center for Problem-Based Learning (PBL), and Linda Torp, Strategic Coordinator for PBL Initiatives, as well as Mary Beth Murphy and Jane Knight who served as coordinators during year 1 of the project to conduct on-site mentoring sessions with the teachers in the fall term and observations and peer coaching sessions for each school team in the spring term.

Schools participating in phase one of this project were selected through an application process that considered commitment to service learning, an interest in problem-based learning, existing collaborative networks, and support for interdisciplinary curricula. See Exhibit 5 for participating schools.

RATIONALE FOR THE PROJECT

Purpose

The nine school teams produced service learning and/problem-based units centered upon a relevant aspect of the waste stream and modeled after the prototype landfill prob-

| Exhibit 5 | List of Participating Schools (All in Illinois) |

School Name and Location	Demographics and Grade
McCleery Accelerated School, Aurora	suburban elementary
Gavin Accelerated School, Chicago Heights	urban elementary
Smyser Accelerated School, Chicago	urban elementary
Batavia Middle School, Batavia	suburban middle school
Sandburg Middle School, Freeport	urban middle school
Thurgood Marshall Middle School, Chicago	urban middle school
Washington Middle School, Springfield	urban middle school
Chicago Vocational Essential School, Chicago	urban high school
Steinmetz Essential School, Chicago	urban high school

lem. These units varied in both focus and presentation. Materials and activities were designed for students in elementary, middle school, or upper grades and in response to different developmental needs and abilities. Each team established its own learning outcomes by considering district outcomes and objectives, state goals for learning, and appropriate national standards.

Research Component

This project involved three different research bases:

First, all school teams were informed by three principles of service learning offered by the National Staff Development Council (NSDC).

□ All involved in the service experience are appropriately prepared, including students, teachers, and community members.

□ The service activity addresses real community issues or needs.

□ Student debriefing and reflection of the experience relates to academic, social, and personal development (NSDC, 1994).

Second, problem-based learning is an educational innovation that organizes curriculum and instruction around carefully crafted "ill-structured" problems. Rather than receiving information first then applying what has been learned, PBL confronts students with a messy situation in which they must identify the real problem and learn whatever is necessary to achieve resolution. This approach has its roots in the work of Howard Barrows (1988) and in the ideas of John Dewey, which focus upon the teaching of thinking and the solving of significant problems.

Problem-based learning as defined by IMSA is a recursive, problem-solving technique that leads to developing habits of mind that support inquiry and data-driven decision-making. Students gather and apply knowledge and skills from multiple disciplines in their search for solutions.

Guided by teachers acting as cognitive coaches, students tackle complexity and engage in meaningful learning.

Third, our model incorporates many elements of coaching. Integrative ways of thinking, problem-handling, and repertoires of different ways of knowing do not just happen because kids meet ill-structured problems. The problem for teachers of problem-based learning is knowing how to maximize the effects they know can come from this approach by good coaching and effective problem design. Coaches ask probing and challenging questions that help students to identify not only their conceptual understanding but also their developing thinking strategies and the role those strategies play in meaning-making. Coached through some false starts, blind alleys, and information "dumps," students come to understand that it is not enough to simply know what an article or an experiment or a community resource says. Coaches also help students to consider how placing that information in the context of the problem alters the significance of the information and how new information may alter the nature of the problem.

Project Features

Each team determined its own local implementation strategy. Nevertheless, in the interest of maximizing the benefits of PBL, all school teams were required to maintain the consistent design and implementation features in their units, indeed, identifying the work as problem-based learning. Features of our PBL model include

☐ introducing the unit by having students assume a role in a complex problem situation. This situation confronted the students with an ill-structured problem that they first defined for themselves and then worked to resolve.

This problem has two parts. First, there is a question about the issue: "How can we advise the mayor of Geneva on the placement of a new landfill?" Second, there is a statement of conditions necessary to adequately resolve the issue: "in such a way that we: (a) honor our contract; (b) respond to community concerns as possible; (c) maintain the safety of the environment to the degree possible; (d) make an economically feasible decision; (e) maintain the integrity of our firm by responding with ethical responsibility?"

◻ The unit concluded with a performance assessment and debriefing in which students presented their resolution to the problem in a setting authentic to their role in the problem and reflected on what they had learned, where their thinking was strongest or weakest, and what learning issues or strategies they needed to address in future work.

◻ Both the materials and learning activities were supportive and adaptive. That is, the students met their problem and were subsequently supported in working toward its resolution throughout. The teaching and learning sequence was designed to

> ◻ help students acknowledge and respond appropriately to the changeable nature of the ill-structured problem and the persisting uncertainty about information surrounding it;

> ◻ develop, test, and refine self-selected plans for action;

> ◻ arrive at their own informed conclusions about the most appropriate (vs. the "right") resolution to the problem.

◻ The design and implementation of the PBL unit highlighted interdisciplinary connections and encouraged students to formulate an integrative, holistic conceptual picture of the problem with which they were confronted. Through a series of concept mapping activities, both teachers and students had various opportunities to visually represent their unfolding picture of the problem and its growing, changing character.

◻ The teaching and learning plan or template (a highly flexible implementation guide) included critical teaching and learning events that unfold in a recursive way in response to the students' learning needs (see Figure 15 in next section).

◻ Each problem had a service learning focus; that is, the problem deliberately blended academic learning with community service. Students learned and applied knowledge and skills to a real-world situation while their communities both contributed to the students' understanding of the problem and then benefited from the products of the students' efforts in bringing that problem to a level of greater understanding or resolution.

THE FLOW OF A Pʙʟ UNIT AND SAMPLE ACTIVITIES

With these guidelines in mind, school teams designed and implemented their PBL units within an organic framework that considers and supports a naturalistic flow from design through implementation (see Figure 12).

The flow of a PBL unit unfolds in an organic way...

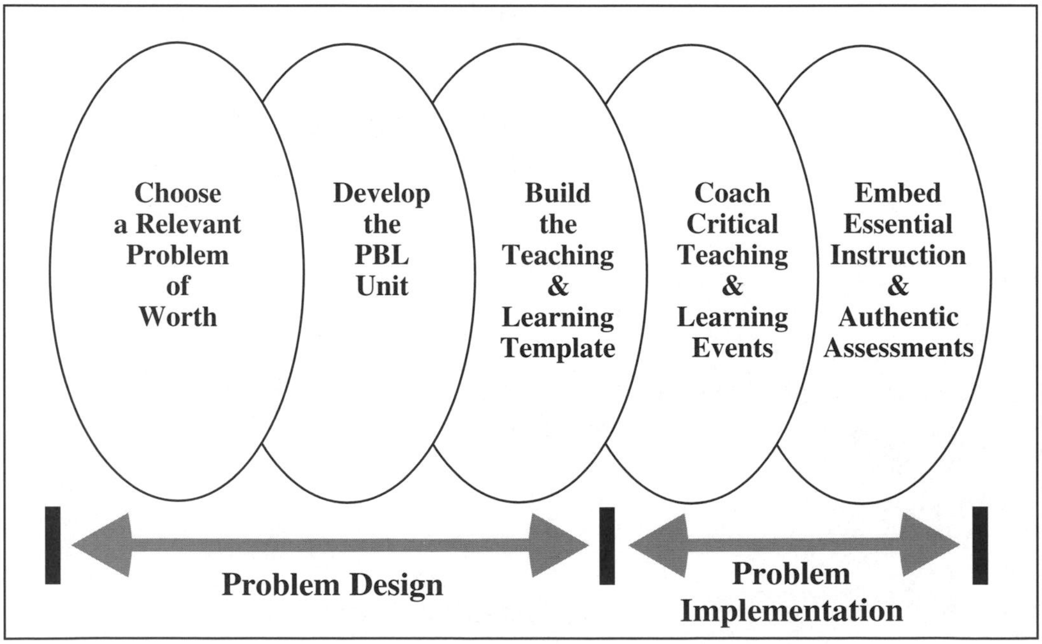

Figure 12 *Flowchart for Illinois Mathematics and Science Academy Problem-Based Learning approach. Copyright by Illinois Mathematics and Science Academy. Used by permission.*

Problem Design

School teams began their design work by considering possibilities for community-based problem situations. Many teachers spoke with officials within their communities, scanned local newspapers for timely stories, and consulted with other community members to identify real problems related to garbage or the waste stream that would serve as the basis for their units. In addition, they kept an eye toward learner characteristics and school curriculum objectives, including their own service learning objectives. This exploration lead to the choice of a relevant problem of worth for students and the community that would provide substantial curricular payback.

To develop the PBL unit they then gave focus to the chosen problem by deciding on a perspective or role and situation through which students will encounter the problem. Which perspective would afford students the greatest opportunity or enticement for engagement? We want students to own the problem, the inquiry, and make a personal investment in the solution. A shift in the perspective through which students meet and understand a problem can have a profound effect upon its resolution. Other aspects of unit development include searching for materials and community resources to enable students' inquiry into the problem, and designing and developing the appropriate materials to support the critical teaching and learning events of PBL.

Building the teaching and learning template requires an appreciation of the teaching and learning events of the PBL process along with an understanding of the role of the teacher as cognitive coach during this implementation process. Through many hours of classroom observation, we have determined the following events to be critical for highly successful PBL experiences.

☐ Teachers may wish to prepare the students for PBL by providing the necessary PBL skills upfront, or skill development may be integrated into subsequent teaching and learning events.

☐ Students meet the problematic situation through the perspective of a stakeholder in the situation. (Note: Student groupings were determined by the teacher teams, so groupings ranged from very large groups to whole classes to small groups.)

☐ Students determine what they know about the situation, what they need to know to the define the problem and come to some resolution, prioritize what needs investigation and learning, and perhaps formulate hypotheses.

☐ Students identify and define the problem inherent in the problematic situation. They write a problem statement which clarifies the issue and the conditions necessary for appropriate resolution.

☐ Students make inquiries and gather information relevant to the problem as defined. They share information gathered to enable all to grasp a holistic understanding of the problem.

☐ Students may revisit what they know and need to know as they learn more about the problem. They may also refine or adjust the problem statement, gather additional information, and discuss an emerging picture of the "real" problem several times before they are ready to generate possible solutions.

☐ Students generate several possible solutions to the problem as defined.

☐ Students evaluate solutions generated in light of the problem statement's identified issue and conditions. They select the solution of best fit.

☐ They offer their solution in an authentic performance situation interacting with real stakeholders in this problem, responding to their questions and concerns, and, if appropriate, implementing the solution in context.

☐ Students and teacher as coach debrief the learning process exposing learning and supporting critical reflection of the process.

As teachers plan or build the template, they have clear goals for each event that relate to student thinking at the cognitive, metacognitive, and epistemic levels.

Problem Implementation

The two phases within problem implementation are very iterative and overlapping. That is, the assessments are embedded throughout the project implementation. Further, within the critical teaching and learning events described above, there are cycles of concept mapping, coaching, re-thinking, and revising.

Periodic embedded assessments of various types not only provide teachers with a sense of the students' developing thinking throughout the teaching and learning sequence but also prompt students to address whole to part and part to whole relationships in the problem. A typical embedded assessment called a problem log may provide previously unknown information and require students to respond to the concerns of people with another perspective (see Exhibit 6).

These problem logs both hold the students in role and prompt them through a real-world quiz format to articulate what they have learned and examine the relationship of that newly-acquired information about social and/or political aspects of the problem to the bigger picture. These assessments build on the students' prior knowledge and encourage integration of old and new knowledge by asking questions such as the following: What is your current thinking as a result of the scientific data you collected? How will the information about social and political concerns contribute to the reconceptualization of the problem?

Concept mapping is another form of periodic embedded assessment that is useful in examining a student's unfolding understanding of the conceptual space of a problem, the interrelationship of ideas, and the relationship of part of the problem to the whole. In comparing concept maps generated at different times, students and teachers both can see how the number of ideas grows over time and how the concepts are reconfigured to illustrate increasingly complex relationships.

Exhibit 6 | **Sample Problem Log**

Sample Problem Log
Fairfax Inn & Restaurant
Geneva, Illinois

October 17, 1994

Michele Barron Pace, C.E.O.
Prairie Environmental Services
1500 West Sullivan Road
Aurora, IL 60506-1000

Dear Dr. Pace:
I am writing this letter as a concerned businesswoman in the Geneva vicinity. As the owner of the Fairfax Inn & Restaurant, I am committed to providing my customers with the highest quality service. I take pride in our motto "Sit Back and Enjoy Yourself," which is considered a guarantee by most of our clients.

It is my understanding that you are surveying different sites in Geneva to determine their suitability for a landfill. One of the identified sites is close to the Fairfax Inn, which is currently being remodeled to include an outdoor fine dining area. I am sure I do not need to tell you what the proximity of a landfill would do to our business. The noise of the transport trucks, safety issues created by heavier traffic, and the stench from the landfill would all be detrimental. I also believe this would be detrimental to our community image as we already have one landfill.

I am interested in learning more about your thinking about the best placement for the site. Please advise me of the effect this landfill would have on my current property value and taxes. Also, I understand that you met with community officials today. What other political/social implications might influence your decision and how will these implications affect the big picture as you have come to view it in your study? I look forward to hearing from you soon.
Sincerely,

Joanne Fairfax
Owner, Fairfax Inn and Restaurant

As students become satisfied with their definition of the problem and begin to focus their attention on building potential solutions and analyzing which solutions best fit the conditions for a good solution, they continue to benefit from graphic organizers that they compose themselves from the raw material of the problem. Grids, matrices, deductive towers, cause and effect fishbones (graphic representations of complex cause and effect interactions), and others devices can help learners to organize their thinking about which potential site would be most appropriate for the mayor of Geneva to consider.

In order to bring the problem to acceptable closure, the students need to not only make a decision but also to provide support for that decision that stands up to the rigors of sound reasoning as well as ethical and moral responsibility. The final performance assessment, like the problem logs, maintains the students' role in order to maximize the authenticity of the assessment. Engaging the real community players in this activity also increases the students' sense of empowerment. As a PBL student once commented, "Hey, this is the real thing, not Mr. T pretending to be on a committee."

Students were most often evaluated in teams during the performance assessment, but they were also evaluated individually through the problem logs and the final concept map. Combining techniques allows teachers to fulfill Illinois state requirements for multiple means of evaluation at multiple points of evaluation. Teachers composed their own rubrics for evaluation with the following general rule: solutions should be evaluated according to their "fit" to the conditions of the problem as determined by the students and not with regard to a predetermined right answer.

As students present their recommendations to community members or officials, their peers sometimes perform their own assessments of the other groups' work, and following their performances, students self-assess using a question guide provided by the coaches. All of this information is brought together in the debriefing session where students examine how the various solutions differed and why, and what the experts thought about the ways in which they handled the problem. Equally important is what the students themselves thought about both the way they handled the problem this time and how they would approach it differently if they were confronted with it again knowing what they now know both about this particular issue and about strategies for handling problems in general. Here as elsewhere the coach's questions can be critical in helping students to think about their thinking.

REFLECTION AND SELF-ASSESSMENT

Learning from Experience

Year 1 of this project proved to be a learning experience for teachers, administrators, students, parents, community members and professional developers alike. Materials developed, reviewed, and polished with the critical eyes of professional educators do not necessarily overcome the challenges of real urban, suburban, and rural classrooms. Students with other concerns, schools operating within traditional schedules, teachers pressed to do more and more with less and less put hurdles in the path of innovation and change. We learned about the power of motivated teachers to jump those hurdles with persistence and flexibility. When altered schedules ate away at time reserved for this project, they found a way. When funding support did not materialize on time, they improvised and looked elsewhere. When colleagues questioned new techniques and students' abilities to cope with complexity, the students came through with high levels of engagement and deep levels of understanding.

As professional developers, we grappled with concurrently training teachers to design and implement PBL units while at the same time training regional coordinators and future trainers of trainers to ensure the same program's longevity. Planning and training days typically lead to regrouping days where previous plans were set aside to meet the needs of our adult learners. The assumptions upon which we had made plans were at times faulty and, at other times, outrageously wrong. In an ideal world, traffic flows normally, it doesn't snow on meeting days, teaching assignments aren't shuffled, everyone views the situation through the same lens, we all hold the same beliefs about teaching and learning, and the check arrives on time. What we relearned is that all schools are different, all teachers are unique individuals, and we are all people of good will.

The action-based, contextual, problem-based learning experiences demanded authentic assessments designed to capture the richness of students' learning or the depths of their misconceptions, while at the same time remaining appropriate to the learning community and the ill-structured problem. Teachers' varying experiences and philosophies of evaluation coupled with our own experiences and philosophies made assessment within the PBL experience and of the PBL experience problematic. This will remain an area in which we will continue to inquire, learn, and progress as this project moves forward.

Year 2 will bring nine more school teams into the project with two additional regional trainer-coordinators. Six school teams from the year 1 cadre will be supported in the continuation of their service learning initiatives. We will continue to support and mentor isbe trainer-coordinators in these efforts. Three of the original nine schools were selected to engage in a more intensive partnership with IMSA's Center for Problem-Based Learning and will begin an action research inquiry into problem based learning's contribution to service learning endeavors.

Reflections of Success

As we reflect upon the outcomes of this phase of this project, we are encouraged by indications of positive change in the way in which both teachers and students are engaged in the learning process. Teachers consciously worked to develop and nurture a classroom community in which students are safe and supported in their inquiry. They have shed the mantle of expert in favor of guide, facilitator, and coinvestigator. Many have reported a new-found trust in their students' desire to learn and a respect for abilities that they had overlooked. One middle school teacher shared that she is ". . . giving ownership back to the students, where it belongs—they own the problem—and the freeing part and the enthusiasm that students brought to it fed me intellectually and it fed me emotionally as a teacher to watch them. . . " (personal communication).

Students are assuming a greater responsibility for their own learning. They have discovered in the authentic, integrative inquiry supported by PBL an energy source that fuels their desire to learn. Students at Washington Middle School in Springfield investigated the school's generation and disposal of solid waste, developed waste reduction ideas, piloted these ideas in three test classrooms, and devised methods to measure the effects of their idea implementation. Solid waste decreased by 40%, reducing waste cartage to the landfill, and Washington students' awareness of solid waste and recycling increased as measured by before and after surveys.

Early in March students at Steinmetz High School in Chicago took ownership of a biomedical hazardous waste disposal problem at Our Lady of Resurrection Medical Center's parking garage. Students worked in departmental teams and investigated the legal, waste management, incineration, public relations, and financial issues of the problem. Opportunities to work in a collegial manner with fellow students and teachers highlights individual strengths and provides apprenticing opportunities to develop in other areas. By the end of April, the proposed problem solution was presented to hospital officials leading to swift problem resolution. Authentic assessments such as this are an essential part of the PBL process, providing specific and timely feedback along the way to support student learning.

Teachers from Batavia Middle School reported that

> For most students this was the first time they were in total control of their learning. While this was an exhilarating experience, it was also frightening. Students were required to learn self-discipline and responsibility in a real-world work setting. (personal communciation)

Although teachers were there to provide direction to resources, students were required to process and communicate information first-hand. From this information, they were to analyze important data and synthesize the evidence presented by such into a reasonable and thoughtful decision. This was perhaps the most difficult for them, as they soon realized that real-world problems are "messy," and that they are not necessarily solved to the benefit of all. Students of all abilities were able to use whatever intelligences were accessible to them, not only to teach themselves but others. They discovered the power within them to educate, advocate, and contribute.

Using problem-based learning as the means to design and implement service learning curricula holds tremendous potential to transform education and nurture a sense of communal responsibility. Students serving as resources to their communities move beyond volunteerism into involvement, rediscovering relevance for learning and finding meaning within the context of community. Teachers in the role of designers and coaches embrace a holistic view of teaching and learning that integrates curriculum and instruction, empowering both teachers and students within the context of learning.

In this activity, we will focus on *Phase 4: Preparing & Presenting Findings* and *Phase 5: Debriefing & Consolidation.*

1a **Understanding the Teacher Authors' PBL-CD Units:** Compare and contrast ideas from the two PBL-CD units. What useful ideas have these teacher authors incorporated into their PBL-CD units? Which ideas are unique to each unit and which are common to both units? Record them in the appropriate areas of this Venn diagram:

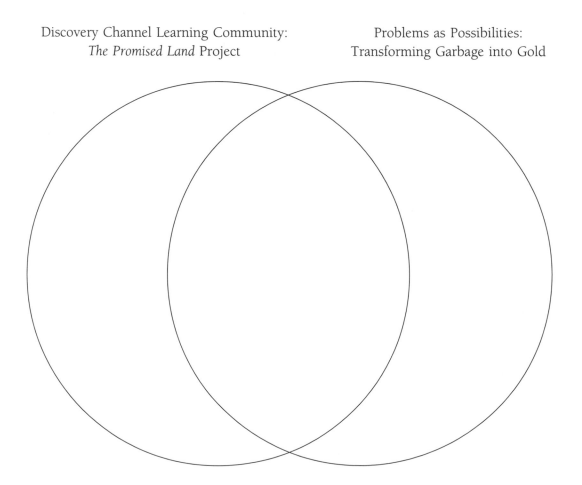

Discovery Channel Learning Community:
The Promised Land Project

Problems as Possibilities:
Transforming Garbage into Gold

1b Understanding and Planning for Your PBL-CD Units: *Phase 4—Preparing and Presenting Findings; and Phase 5—Debriefing and Consolidation.* Using Goal 3 and Appendix C as references, what ideas from the Venn would be most useful to you as you build upon plans in preparation for Phase 4 and 5?

Think about how these ideas and ideas from earlier units will help you to prepare for Phase 4 and 5 of progressive problem solving in the classroom: What teaching and learning strategies will help you and your students identify specific problems? What teacher roles and student roles will be most appropriate throughout this phase?

Teacher Roles	Teaching Goals and Strategies	Student Roles	Learning Strategies and Responsibilities

2 **Acting and Sharing**: When you have completed a draft of possible instructional activities for Phase 4 and 5, share your ideas with a "critical friend" team. Describe your plans for your informal conference below.

Process for a "critical friend" dialogue:

☐ share your desired outcome for the conversation
☐ ask your critical friend to practice active listening and ask clarifying questions
☐ offer constructive, nonjudgmental feedback

3 **Reflecting**: Reflect upon the outcomes of your critical friend conference. List or in some way represent them (metaphor, graphic organizer, icon).

4 **Rethinking and Refining**: What are the implications for you or your team's unit plan?

final review

"Start small, think big."

— Michael Fullan (1993)

You have read stories of innovation, of changes in roles and relationships, and of struggles and triumphs. These stories represent the diverse ways in which practitioners have used interdisciplinary, problem-based learning in schools and communities.

Their search for more meaningful learning and teaching began with reflections on practice. These teachers then improved their practice by engaging in a progressive process of curriculum development: continually understanding and planning for problem-based learning; acting on their plans and sharing their results; reflecting on their work; and rethinking and refining their work.

Teaching and learning in their schools and communities as well as their own professional growth was further strengthened by collaboration. Groups of students became more engaged in their own real-life problem solving. Students, teachers, practitioners-in-the-field, and community members became more frequent coinvestigators, coproducers, and coevaluators. Teachers benefited from the feedback and support of critical friends while developing and implementing curricula.

Problem-Based Learning as Codevelopment provided a framework for improving practice, enhancing student learning, and contributing to the knowledge base around problem solving. PBL-CD has been a powerful experience for us as well as the practitioners we have worked with. In creating this framework with the people using it in schools, we have been able to combine research and best practice in a way that engages teachers in the same collaborative approach to interdisciplinary, real-life problem solving that we espouse for students. The authentic work of codeveloping PBL curricula has provided structure to our changing roles and relationships and has advanced the work of an ever-expanding community of practice.

We hope that you have found meaning in the content of this book and that by engaging in the self-directed activities, you have indeed joined the community of practice around interdisciplinary, problem-based learning. We recognize that changes in practice as complex as PBL take time and that it is often best to start small. Therefore, we asked you to choose a single instructional practice to change before selecting a unit to further develop or refine. We encouraged you to begin to make changes as an individual teacher, but to involve colleagues early on in the curriculum development process as critical friends and members of your design team. Step by step, we guided you through a planning process so that this complex innovation would be more manageable. Finally, we provided plenty of actual examples of real-life problem solving so that you could consider a variety of applications when planning.

Now we hope that you feel ready to implement your PBL unit. In fact, we think that engaging in problem-based learning by actually doing an investigation of a real problem is essential for further curriculum development. This is especially true if units involve students in the choice of problems, in planning for and carrying out an investigation, in creating products and presenting findings, and in evaluating their learning. Your students will in many ways be the best judges of the PBL unit. They will be able to let you know early in the unit whether or not the problems and tasks are truly meaningful to them. Over the course of the unit, their triumphs and struggles will provide information about ways to better manage a challenging investigation. Together you can continue to refine your unit—learning by doing.

When thinking about the importance of collaboration and learning by doing to next steps in your PBL unit, we are reminded of the advice of Michael Fullan (1993). When talking about curriculum development and implementation, he advocated that educators

> start into action as soon as possible establishing small scale examples, adapting, refining, improving quality, expanding, and reshaping as the process unfolds. This strategy might be summed up as start small, think big: or the way to get better at implementation planing is more by doing than by planning.(p. 27)

We feel that his advice is essential to the development and implementation of real-life problem solving.

We hope that Problem-Based Learning as Codevelopment will continue to facilitate sound professional development and support change over time by providing a comprehensive framework and tools for thoughtful curricular planning and an ongoing process for implementation.

We have been inspired by the diverse and powerful ways in which reflective practitioners make PBL-CD happen in schools and communities and by the extraordinary impact of such learning on students. The creativity and commitment of students and of teachers, like those described in this book and like you, reinforce our desire to start small yet think big when engaging in real-life problem solving.

appendix a

Indicators of
Engaged Learning

Variable	Indicator of Engaged Learning	Indicator Definition
Vision of Learning	Responsible for learning	Learner involved in setting goals, choosing tasks, developing assessments and standards for the tasks; has big picture of learning and next steps in mind.
	Strategic	Learner actively develops repertoire of thinking/learning strategies.
	Energized by learning	Learner is not dependent on rewards from others; has a passion for learning.
	Collaborative	Learner develops new ideas and understanding in conversations and work with others.
Tasks	Authentic	Pertains to real world, may be addressed to personal interest.
	Challenging	Difficult enough to be interesting but not totally frustrating, usually sustained.
	Multidisciplinary	Involves integrating disciplines to solve problems and address issues.
Assessment	Performance-based	Involving a performance or demonstration, usually for a real audience and useful purpose.
	Generative	Assessments having meaning for learner; maybe produce information, product, service.
	Seamless and ongoing	Assessment is part of instruction and vice versa; students learn during assessment.
	Equitable	Assessment is culture fair.
Instructional Model	Interactive	Teacher or technology program responsive to student needs, requests (e.g., menu driven).
	Generative	Instruction oriented to constructing meaning; providing meaningful activities and experiences.
Learning Context	Collaborative	Instruction conceptualizes students as part of learning community; activities are collaborative.
	Knowledge-building	Learning experiences set up to bring multiple perspectives to solve problems such that each perspective contributes to shared understanding for all; goes beyond brainstorming.
	Empathetic	Learning environment and experiences set up for valuing diversity, multiple perspectives, strengths.
Grouping	Heterogeneous	Small groups with persons from different ability levels and backgrounds.
	Equitable	Small groups organized so that over time all students have challenging learning tasks/experiences.
	Flexible	Different groups organized for different instructional purposes so each person is a member of different groups; works with different people.
Teacher Roles	Facilitator	Engaged in negotiation, stimulates and monitors discussion and project work but does not control.
	Guide	Helps students to construct their own meaning by modeling, mediating, explaining when needed, redirecting focus, providing options.
	Co-learner/co-investigator	Teacher considers self as learner; willing to take risks to explore areas outside his or her expertise; collaborates with other teachers and practicing professionals.

Student Roles	Explorer	Students have opportunities to explore new ideas/tools; push the envelope in ideas and research.
	Cognitive Approaches	Learning is situated in relationship with mentor who coaches students to develop ideas and skills that simulate the role of practicing professionals (i.e., engage in real research).
	Teacher	Students encouraged to teach others in formal and informal contexts.
	Producer	Students develop products of real use to themselves and others.

Source: Jones, B., Valdez, G., Nowakowski, J., & Rasmussen, C. (1995). *Plugging in: Choosing and using educational technology.* Washington DC: Council for Educational Development and Research. Copyright B. Jones, C. Rasmussen, and M. Moffitt. (1995). North Central Regional Educational Laboratory, Oak Brook, IL. Reprinted by permission.

appendix b

PBL-CD Template:
Outcomes and Assessments

PBL-CD Unit: _____ Phase: _____ Timeframe: _____

Class Broad Task(s) and Problem(s): _____

Inquiry Groups & Open-Ended Questions: _____

DISCIPLINES & ELEMENTS	OUTCOMES: specific concepts/strategies/skills	STANDARDS/ASSESSMENTS: methods/tools/strategies and criteria for success	PBL PHASE

Note: Copyright B. Jones, C. Rasmussen, and M. Moffitt. (1995). North Central Regional Educational Laboratory, Oak Brook, IL. Used by permission.

appendix c

PBL-CD: An Illustration of the
PBL-CD Teaching and Learning Process

Identifying Specific Problems

Possible Teacher Roles	Teaching Strategies/Goals	Possible Student Roles	Learning Strategies/Responsibilities	Flexible Grouping
Facilitator/Guide	Explain broad task and open-ended problem/question. Use guided questioning to ensure understanding. Invite students to brainstorm.	Problem Solver	Discuss prior knowledge and interests. Ask questions.	Whole Group
Facilitator/Guide	Guide students to categorize, consider multiple perspectives, and map concepts/perspectives.	Problem Solver	Reflect on possible inquiry topics, and prioritize interests. Consider possible paths of inquiry, products, services, and goals.	WholeGroup/Small Groups
Planner (Mentally)/Planner	Check student reflections against broad task, problem, and curricular goals/outcomes. Establish inquiry groups, ideally with students.	Coplanner	Establish interest groups.	Small Groups
Colearner/Model	Collaborate with students to set goals, define specific problems/inquiry.	Problem Solver/Collaborator	Develop specific problems/open-ended questions.	Small Groups
Guide/Model	Guide students to identify and practice needed collaborative/social skills. Invite students to consider and plan for self-assessment and record keeping. Suggest various options.	Planner/Producer	Develop guidelines for collaboration. Practice collaborative/social skills, if needed. Discuss purposes of self-assessment as well as different types. Discuss rubrics and generate self-assessment.	Whole Group

Developing a Plan of Inquiry/Work

Possible Teacher Roles	Teaching Strategies/Goals	Possible Student Roles	Learning Strategies/ Responsibilities	Flexible Grouping
Colearner/Model	Collaborate with students (1) to consider possible solutions to problems and (2) examine available and needed resources within and beyond the classroom.	Problem Solver/ Collaborator	Formulate different points of view, theories, hypotheses. Consider alternatives solutions, paths of inquiry, goals.	Small Groups
Facilitator/ Colearner/Guide	Guide students to generate ideas for appropriate products/actions. Elicit goals and benchmarks for inquiry. Encourage student assessment of collaborative skills. Broker resources.	Problem Solver/ Planner	Define goals and formulate general plan for inquiry. Establish goals for final product or action, and criteria for progress and success.	Small Groups
Planner (Mentally)	Check student plans and potential learnings against curricular goals/parameters. Anticipate needs.	Planner/Decision Maker	Assign small group roles and work.	Small Groups
Manager/Guide/ Colearner	Guide students to share and coordinate plans/use of resources. Develop graphics for each group and/or whole group with students.	Collaborator/Critical Friend/Evaluator	Each group shares plans, adjusts and revises according to feedback from teacher and peers.	Whole Group

Conducting the Inquiry and Analysis

Possible Teacher Roles	Teaching Strategies/Goals	Possible Student Roles	Learning Strategies/ Responsibilities	Flexible Grouping
Monitor/Model/ Facilitator	Watch progress of group investigations, model inquiry skills, and help students develop hypotheses.	Colearner/Explorer/ Problem Solver	Each group plumbs resources and begins to formulate hypotheses as sketches, notes, drafts, etc.	Small Groups
Facilitator/Manager/ Model	Invite groups to share preliminary ideas with Groups another group that plays role of critical friend or collaborator or with whole group and/or on file sharing software.	Reflective Learner/ Critical Friend/ Apprentice	All groups share early work with others. Each group responds to early findings of others. Discuss/broker additional resources. May communicate with local and/or global experts.	Whole Group/ Small
Planner (Mentally)/ Monitor	Check activities against curricular goals/outcomes. May modify them or redirect students, as appropriate. Make sure each group is working with big ideas.	Problem Solver/ Evaluator	Groups revise/modify their thinking and may redirect activities/goals/problem definition.	Small Groups
Facilitator/Guide/ Coach	Monitor group work. Anticipate new needs for Group resources and help. May guide groups through continued knowledge	Critical Friend/ Collaborator	Groups communicate new research/ideas to critical friend.	Small Groups/ Whole

Preparing and Presenting Findings

Possible Teacher Roles	Teaching Strategies/Goals	Possible Student Roles	Learning Strategies/Responsibilities	Flexible Grouping
Monitor/Model/Coach	Monitor findings. May work with specific groups to help them solve problems and refine ideas.	Producer/Problem Solver	Begin to construct drafts or models for final product(s). Refine hypotheses, and theories, synthesize findings from multiple sources/perspectives.	Small Groups
Planner (Mentally)/Monitor	Check investigations, findings, and benchmarks against curricular goals/outcomes. May modify curriculum or redirect group work.	Critical Friend/Evaluator	Share drafts with critical friends, teachers, and experts. Clarify ideas, returning to active investigation as needed. Review for multiple perspectives.	Small Groups/Whole Group
Guide/Monitor	Invite students to plan for assessment event or presentation. Monitor to help students work through alternative approaches and compare assessment with criteria for success. Check products	Producer/Problem Solver/Evaluator	Plan for final presentation. Set up logistics for actual presentations. Check back with identified benchmarks. Review materials to make sure multiple perspectives and all plans are covered.	Whole Group/Small Groups
Facilitator/Monitor	Monitor rehearsals, especially to make sure each group focuses on big ideas and builds on strengths of all group members.	Producer/Teacher/Evaluator	Each group finalizes details for presentations, rehearses with other groups and/or with teacher, and revises performance as needed	Small Groups
Manager/Guide/Evaluator	Monitor each presentation for quality and for questioning for audience. Guide audience questions as needed.	Producer/Teacher	Make final presentation(s) to one or more audience.	Small Groups/Whole Group

Debriefing and Consolidating

Teacher Role	Instructional Strategy/Goals	Student Role	Student Activities	Grouping
Guide/Monitor	Invite each group to gather feedback from audience(s).	Reflective Learner/ Evaluator	Gather and reflect on feedback from audience(s).	Small Groups
Guide/Evaluator	Invite each group to debrief its own performance as well as those of other groups.	Producer/Teacher/ Evaluator	Groups critique themselves orally and/or in writing. Discuss ways to improve.	Small Groups
Guide/Evaluator	Debrief lessons collaboratively with students covering content, skills, inquiry methods, resources, transfer, and next steps.	Producer/Teacher/ Evaluator	Articulate concepts, skills, and methods learned. Discuss final overall learnings. Consider connections and possible next steps.	Whole Group

Note: Copyright B. Jones, C. Rasmussen, and M. Moffitt. (1995). North Central Regional Educational Laboratory, Oak Brook, IL. Used by permission.

☐ Brainstorming and organizing ideas via any of many group recording strategies (e.g., KWHL, etc.).

☐ Questioning to elicit problems, understanding, perspectives, hypotheses, and plans.

☐ Thinking/pairing/sharing and other similar strategies to ensure oral participation of everyone.

☐ Keeping journal or other written strategies to identify individual student's interests and his or her understanding of the problem, plans for inquiry, research, and feedback.

☐ Concept mapping and other graphical representations around a problem and the growing knowledge of it.

☐ Representing in writing or graphically an understanding of broad goals and framework for the problem-solving process.

☐ Modeling and simulating skills for collaboration and inquiry.

☐ Student and teacher-generated peer review forms for feedback from others to incorporate in refinements of plans for investigation.

☐ Student and teacher-generated assessment tools for own use and possibly audience use (e.g., checklist, rubric, interview, journal entry).

glossary

Action research—practitioners ask research-based questions of interest to them, design activities to address the questions, and make observations that inform their theories of learning and their practice. In this way, teachers engage in inquiry to study what they are doing.

Alternative assessments—includes any type of assessment in which students create a response to a question rather than choose a response from a given list (e.g., multiple-choice, true/false, or matching). Alternative assessments can include short answer questions, essays, performances, oral presentations, demonstrations, exhibitions, and portfolios.

Authentic tasks—activities for learners that represent tasks, issues, or problems in the real world—often including their complexities, ambiguities, messy data, inadequate information, opportunities, and multiple perspectives. Authentic tasks involve contexts and audiences that are meaningful to the learner.

Codevelopment—activities that involve people in designing and implementing something together. PBL-CD emphasizes the codevelopment of curriculum (a) between professional developers and teachers; (b) among teachers; (c) between teacher and students; and (d) among teachers, students, and the broader research and development community.

Cognitive apprenticeship—teaching and learning are situated in authentic contexts. Teachers act as coaches and mentors while students become cognitive apprentices who learn concepts and academic skills from teachers in much the same ways that apprentices learn from masters in the crafts.

Community of practice—engagement in the practice, not proximity or similarity of work or function, defines the community. The norms that emerge from common goals, shared work, and from sustained interactions over time hold the community together and distinguish it from some other teams, groups, work units, and networks.

Critical friends—colleagues, classmates, or others who provide helpful feedback and stimulate reflection and refinement of work. In PBL-CD, critical friends provide only constructive feedback, without judging; listen actively, taking time to understand the "big picture" and the process of planning or implementing; and advocate for the success of the work.

Debriefing—at significant points in a learning process, teachers and students identify learnings, make connections among learnings, and synthesize learnings. When debriefing, they may revisit earlier predictions, hypotheses, and theories and make revisions as well as consider implications, applications, and next steps.

Engaged learning—learners take an active role in meaningful tasks and activities. Highly engaged learners take increasing responsibility for their own learning, striving for deep understanding through experiences that directly apply to their lives. (See Appendix A for indicators of engaged learning.)

Flexible grouping—teachers group and regroup students according to the purposes of instruction. In a problem-based study, much of the grouping alternates between whole group activities and the ongoing work of small interest or skill groups.

Graphic representations—tables, flow charts, Venn diagrams, cycles, concept maps, semantic webs, and other visual organizers of text.

Interdisciplinary—teaching and learning that addresses concepts and skills from more than one discipline.

Knowledge building—constructing meaning by making connections between new information (facts, concepts, principles, etc.) and prior knowledge and experiences.

Multiple intelligences—theory, developed by Howard Gardner, that proposes that there are at least seven intelligences valued by society: verbal-linguistic, mathematical-deductive reasoning, kinesthetic, spatial, musical, interpersonal, and intrapersonal.

Open-ended problems and questions—open-ended questions, often referred to as ill-structured problems, have no single correct response or simple answer. These problems or questions often involve: messy data that may be incomplete, inconsistent, and ambiguous; multiple perspectives; limited time; multiple disciplines; and various resources and modes of inquiry.

Performance-based assessments—evaluation that measures the quality of student performance on a task. In PBL, alternative assessments are often used to evaluate both the process and the final products or presentation of an investigation.

Problem-based learning—teachers and students integrate concepts and skills from one or more disciplines while investigating a problem. PBL often engages students in the development of a relatively long-term project.

Problem-Based Learning as Codevelopment—PBL-CD is a framework for professional development and curriculum development. It is based on the belief that people build expertise in problem-based teaching and learning by using a progressive problem solving approach to tasks and problems of importance to them and by designing and implementing curriculum together.

Progressive problem solving—process of solving problems in which people continuously rethink and redefine their tasks, always striving to build knowledge and do better. In PBL-CD learners engage in four fundamental thinking processes repeatedly throughout their work: understanding and planning an application; acting on their plan and sharing their results; reflecting on their work; and rethinking and refining the work.

Student roles—in PBL, students often assume varied roles including those of explorer, cognitive apprentice, teacher, and producer. As *explorers*, students have opportunities to explore new ideas and tools, as well as "push the envelope" in ideas and research. As *cognitive apprentices*, learning is situated in relationship with a mentor who coaches students to develop ideas and skills that simulate the role of practicing professionals (i.e., engage in real research). As *teachers*, students are encouraged to teach others in formal and informal contexts. In the role of *producers*, students develop products of real use to themselves and others.

Teacher roles—in PBL, teachers often assume varied roles including those of facilitator, guide, and colearner and coinvestigator. As *facilitators*, teachers engage in negotiation, stimulate and monitor discussion and project work but do not control all the information or direct all the learning. In the role of *guide*, teachers help students to construct their own meaning by modeling, mediating, explaining when needed, redirecting focus, and providing options. As *colearner* and *co-investigators*, teachers consider themselves learners; willing to take risks to explore areas outside their expertise; they collaborate with other teachers and practicing professionals.

references

Abbott, J. (1995). Children need communities—communities need children. *Educational Leadership, 52*(8), 6–10.

Academy One. Available:
http://www.nptn.org/cyber.serv/AOneP

Altwerger, B., Edelsky, C., & Flores, B. M. (1987). Whole language: What's new? *The Reading Teacher, 41*(2), 144–154.

APA Presidential Task Force on Psychology and Education. (1993, January). *Learner-centered psychological principles: Guidelines for school redesign and reform.* Washington, DC: American Psychological Association; Aurora, CO: Mid-continent Regional Educational Laboratory.

Aronson, E. (1978). *The jigsaw classroom.* Beverly Hills, CA: Sage Publications.

Barrows, H. (1986). A taxonomy of problem-based learning methods. *Medical Education, 20,* 481–486.

Barrows, H. S. (1988). *The tutorial process.* Springfield, IL: Southern Illinois University School of Medicine.

Bereiter, C., & Scardamalia, M. (1993). *Surpassing ourselves: An inquiry into the nature and implications of expertise.* Chicago: Open Court.

Berenfeld, B. (1993). A moment of glory in San Antonio: A Global Lab story. *Hands on!, 6*(2), 1, 19–21.

Blumenfeld, P. C., Soloway, E., Marx, R. W., Krajcik, J. S., Guzdial, M., & Palincsar, A. (1991). Motivating project-based learning: Sustaining the doing, supporting the learning. *Educational Psychologist, 26*(3 & 4), 369–398.

B'nai B'rith, Television / Film / Radio Dept., Anti-Defamation League. (1981). *The american story.* New York: Author

Bolt, Beranek, and Newman, Inc. (1993). *The Co-NECT school: design for a new generation of american schools.* Cambridge, MA: Author.

Brady, M., Munroe, W., & Rasmussen, C. (1987). Reflecting the world around us: Building multicultural understanding. *Pupil Enrichment Program Curriculum Guide.* Wilmette, IL: Avoca District #37.

Bridges, E. M., & Hallinger, P. (1992). *Problem-based learning for administrators.* Eugene, OR: ERIC Clearinghouse on Educational Management, University of Oregon.

Brooks, J. G., & Brooks, M. G. (1993). *In search of understanding: The case for constructivist classrooms.* Alexandria, VA: Association for Supervision and Curriculum Development.

Burke, K. (1994). *The mindful school: How to access authentic learning.* Palentine, IL: Skylight Publishing, Inc.

Caine, R. N., & Caine G. (1994). *Making Connections: Teaching and the human brain.* Alexandria, VA: Association for Supervision and Curriculum Development.

Carnegie Council on Adolescent Development. (1989). *Turning points: Preparing American youth for the 21st century.* New York: Carnegie Corporation of New York.

Checkoway, B., & Flynn, J. (1992). *Young people as community builders.* Ann Arbor, MI: Center for the Study of Youth Policy, School for Social Work, University of Michigan.

Coalition for Essential Schools. Available: http://aisr.ces.brown.edu/ces/first.html

Cognition and Technology Group at Vanderbilt (CTGV). (1992). The Jasper Series as an example of anchored instruction: Theory, program description, and assessment data. *Educational Psychologist, 27*(3), 201–315.

Collins, A., Brown, J. S., & Holum, A. (1991, Winter). Cognitive apprenticeship: Making thinking visible [Special Edition]. *American Educator,* pp. 6–11, 38–46.

Cognition and Technology Group at Vanderbilt. (1992). The Jasper Series as an example of anchored instruction: Theory, program description, and assessment data. *Educational Psychologist, 27*(3), 201–315.

Costa, A. L., & Kallick, B. (1993). Through the lens of a critical friend. *Educational Leadership, 52*(2), 49–51.

Cummins, J. (1986). *Bilingualism and minority-language children.* Toronto, Canada: OISE Press.

Feldman, A., & McWilliams (1995). *Planning guide for network science.* Cambridge, MA: TERC Communications.

Finkle, S., Briggs, R., Hinton, L., Thompson, J., & Dods, R. (1994). *The summer challenge landfill problem.* Aurora, IL: Illinois Math and Science Academy.

Flower, L., & Hayes, J. R. (1994). The cognition of discovery: Defining a rhetorical problem. In S. Perl (Ed.), *Landmark essays on writing process* (pp. 63–74). Davis, CA: Hermagoras Press.

Fullan, M. (1993). *"What's worth fighting for in the principalship?"* (Monograph). Ontario, Canada: Ontario Public School Teachers' Federation.

Gardner, H. (1990). *Art education and human development.* (Occasional Paper 3). Los Angeles, CA: Getty Center for Education in the Arts.

Gardner, H. (1991). *The unschooled mind: How children think and how schools should teach.* New York: Basic Books.

Gardner, H. (1993). *Frames of mind: The theory of multiple intelligences.* New York: Basic Books.

Goodman, K. (1986). *What's whole language? A parent/teacher guide to children's learning.* Portsmouth, NH: Heinemann Educational Books.

Graves, M. F. (1982). *The classroom teacher's role in reading instruction in the intermediate and secondary grades.* Minneapolis, MN: University of Minnesota.

Illinios State Board of Education. (1993). An overview of IGAP performance standards for reading, mathematics, writing, science, & social studies. Springfieild, IL: Author.

Information Task Force, Committee on Applications and Technology. (1994). *A transformation of learning: Using the NII for education and lifelong learning* (Draft for Public Comment).

Jacobs, H. H. (1989). *Interdisciplinary curriculum: Design and implementation.* Alexandria, VA: Association for Supervision and Curriculum Development.

Johnson, D., Johnson, R., & Holubec, E. (1988). *Cooperation in the classroom.* Edina, MN: Interaction Book Company.

Jones, B. F. (1992). Cognitive designs in education. In M. C. Alkin (Ed. in Chief), *Encyclopedia of Educational Research* (6th Ed.). New York: Macmillan.

Jones, B. F., Pierce, J., & Hunter, B. (1988). Teaching students to construct graphic representations. *Educational Leadership, 46*(4), 20, 25.

Jones, B. F., Rasmussen, C., & Moffitt, M. (Eds.). (1996). *Transformations: High school reform to promote student performance.* Oak Brook, IL: The North Central Regional Educational Laboratory.

Jones, B. F., Valdez, G., Nowakowski, J., & Rasmussen, C. (1994). *Designing learning and technology through educational reform.* Oak Brook, IL: North Central Regional Educational Laboratory.

Jones, B. F., Valdez, G., Nowakowski, J. & Rasmussen, C. (1995). *Plugging in: Choosing and using educational technology.* Oak Brook, IL: North Central Regional Educational Laboratory.

Jones, R. (1995). Wake up! *Executive Educator, 17*(8), 14–18.

Kasak, D. (1996). Interdisciplinary team organization. In B. F. Jones, C. Rasmussen, & M. Moffitt (Eds.), *Transformations: High school reform to promote student performance* (pp. 10–13). Oak Brook, IL: North Central Regional Educational Laboratory.

Kinsley, C. W., & McPherson, K. (1995). *Enriching the curriculum through service learning.* Alexandria, VA: Association for Supervision and Curriculum Development.

Means, B., Blando, J., Olson, K., Middleton, T., Morocco, C. C., Remz, A. R., & Zorfass, J. (1993). *Using technology to support education reform.* Washington, DC: Office of Educational Research and Improvement, U.S. Department of Education.

Moll, L., & Greenberg, J. B. (1990). Creating zones of possibilities: Combining social contexts for instruction. In L. C. Moll (Ed.), *Vygotsky and education* (pp. 319–348). New York: Cambridge Press.

National Council for the Social Studies Task Force on Ethnic Studies Curriculum Guidelines. (1991). *Curriculum guidelines for multicultural education.* Washington, DC: Author.

National Staff Development Council. (1994). *National Staff Development Council's standards for staff development* (pp. 49–50). Oxford, OH: Author.

Pfister, L. A. (1993). An introduction to LabNet. In R. Ruopp (Ed.), *LabNet: Toward a community of practice* (Chapter 1). Hillsdale, NJ: Erlbaum.

Pfister, L. A. (1993). From current practice to projects. In R. Ruopp (Ed.), *LabNet: Toward a community of practice* (Chapter 2). Hillsdale, NJ: Erlbaum.

Prentice Hall, Inc. (1989). *Prentice Hall Literature.* Needham Heights, MD: Prentice Hall School Division.

Scardamalia, M., & Bereiter, C. (1992, April). Computer-support for knowledge building communities. In P. Feltovich (Chair), *Instructional theories underlying the use of networked computers in the classroom.* Symposium conducted at the annual meeting of the American Educational Research Association, San Francisco.

Scardamalia, M., & Bereiter, C. (in press). Computer support for knowledge-building communities. *Journal of the Learning Sciences.*

Schoenstein, R. (1995). The new school on the block. *Executive Editor, 17*(8), 18–21.

Secretary's Commission on Achieving Necessary Skills (scans), U. S. Department of Labor. (1992). *Learning a liv-*

ing: *A blueprint for high performance* (A SCANS report for America 2000). Washington, DC: Author.

Steinberg, L., Blinde, P. L., & Chan, K. (1982). Dropping out among minority youth. *Review of Educational Research, 54,* 113–132.

Sylwester, R. (1995). *A celebration of neurons.* Alexandria, VA: Association for Supervision and Curriculum Development.

Taylor, A. (1975). Spectrum: *A simulation of ethnic group interaction during a student government election.* Lakeside, CA: Interact Company.

Tinker, P. F. (1993). Curriculum development and the scientific method [Entire issue]. *Hands-On Math and Science Learning, 16*(2).

Vygotsky, L. S. (1978). *Mind in society: The development of higher psychological processes.* Cambridge, MA: Harvard University Press.

Wengler, E. (1995). *Communities of practice: Learning, meaning, and identity.* New York: Cambridge Press.

Wheatley, M. (1992). *Leadership and the new science: Learning about organizations in an orderly universe.* San Francisco: Berrett-Koehler Publishers.

Willis, S. (1992, November). Interdisciplinary learning: Movement to link the disciplines gains momentum [Entire issue]. *ASCD Curriculum Update.*

Willis, S. (1994). Teaching across disciplines: Interest remains high despite concerns over coverage. *ASCD Update, 36*(10), 1, 3–5.

Willis, S. (1995). Refocusing the curriculum: Making interdisciplinary efforts work. *ASCD Education Update, 37*(1), 1, 3, 8.

Willis, S. (1995, Fall). Whole language: Finding the surest way to literacy [Entire issue]. *ASCD Curriculum Update.*

Woods, D. (1994). *How to gain the most from problem-based learning.* Hamilton, Ontario: Author.

Woods, D. (1995). *Problem-based learning: Helping your students gain the most from PBL.* Hamilton, Ontario: Author.

ABOUT THE AUTHORS

Beau Fly Jones is Director, Educational Programs, at Ohio Supercomputer Center. Formerly she was Senior Researcher at the North Central Regional Educational Laboratory, Oak Brook, Illinois, where she worked with practitioners and colleagues to improve reading and thinking in the content areas, to focus school reform on learning, and to build communities of practice around problem-based learning. She received her PhD from Northwestern University in Educational Psychology, specializing in developing learning strategies for students at risk. Her work for two decades focused on developing research-based curricula for classroom use and professional development. More recently, her work has focused on the intersection of teaching, learning, technology use, and policy.

Claudette M. Rasmussen is a Program Associate with the Teaching, Learning, and Curriculum Center at the North Central Regional Educational Laboratory, Oak Brook, IL. She has an MEd from National Louis University and 18 years of experience in schools in the areas of program, curriculum and professional development within special, regular, and gifted education. Throughout her career, Claudette has been interested in the integration of thinking skills into content and the integration of curriculum development into professional development. More recently her work has focused on the nature of learning and the ways in which curriculum design and technology use can support meaningful learning.

Mary C. Moffitt is the Director of Learning Technologies for Schaumburg Community Consolidated Schools (District 54) in Illinois. She has an MA in Reading and Learning Disabilities and has completed advanced work in social and emotional disorders and educational leadership. Mary has been interested in the learning process and how various teaching practices and school systems can be utilized to enhance student learning. She has been actively involved in professional development related to integrating technology across the curriculum. She has done consulting work with schools and has written about the process of technology planning to enhance active and engaged learning.